Governance, Ignorance, and Archives

Keiji Fujiyoshi
Editor

# Governance, Ignorance, and Archives

## Sharing Critical Information in Contemporary Japanese Society

Springer

*Editor*
Keiji Fujiyoshi
Faculty of Sociology
Otemon Gakuin University
Ibaraki-shi, Osaka, Japan

ISBN 978-981-95-1961-3 ISBN 978-981-95-1962-0 (eBook)
https://doi.org/10.1007/978-981-95-1962-0



This Springer imprint is published by the registered company Springer Nature Singapore Pte Ltd.
The registered company address is: 152 Beach Road, #21-01/04 Gateway East, Singapore 189721, Singapore

# Preface

This book explores the current situation of record keeping and archives in Japan. It mainly focuses on the historical, cultural and social background of handling as well as mishandling of records in the public sectors. It also examines how a set of quantitative data is utilized in a society where the religious knowledge has a significant role for political and public decisions.

Japan is well known as a nation of literature, or more correctly, a nation of written language. Around sixth century, Chinese characters were introduced to Japan, and they began to be used to transcribe the sounds of Japanese language, and the oldest records of ancient matters were edited and authorized with those characters by the then dynasty. Those Chinese characters are called "Man'yo-gana." And then, based on those Chinese characters, Japanese people created a unique phonetic lettering system of "hiragana" and "katakana," and it enabled more people to be accustomed to writing.

Written matters are sometimes respected but regarded not so important the other times. Where to draw the line between important and unimportant is one of our research questions. Generally speaking, written matters, especially those which are shared by several stakeholders are a kind of contract that stipulates the conducts of those involved. Contracts are in force only when all of those involved regard them as "contracts" among them. In a modern society, however, there are multiple and complicated rules that control our conduct, and we sometimes get lost about which we are the stakeholder of. Being a citizen in a certain society means being a stakeholder of the governance of the society and the government of the state in accordance. But how can we be a good stakeholder of our society? The book explores the question in several field of a society taking Japan as an example.

Chapter 1 overviews some scandals related to the record-keeping of the Japanese government and draws some insights about what should be recognized by Japanese people in order to refrain such scandals from happening. It underlines that record-keeping and archives is an indispensable instrument for the people to keep their government transparent and compliant. Chapter 2 discusses the development and shortcomings of records management laws in contemporary Japan. By highlighting the democratic function of archives, it maintains their fuller integration into information law frameworks. Chapter 3 begins its exploration by recognizing that only less than one-seventh of the national constitutions mention archives explicitly. It shows these references to archives are categorized into four categories: Rights, Authority and Duty, Value, and Existence. In Chap. 4, the history of creation and development of the concept "governance archives" is clarified in relation to the history of governmental archives in Germany. And then, it provides overview of the status of the development of local government archives in Japan and shows some efforts to ensure the functions of governance archives.

Those four chapters explore the current and recent condition of the record-keeping and archives of the state and local government. Of course, well-managed record-keeping and archives are indispensable for keeping the government transparent and accountable. There should be, however, the laws and rules which regulate the record creating and keeping activities of the government, and also, the public who pay close attention to their government's activities on the basis of the governmental records. Paying attention and controlling activities on the basis of records is a kind of social and cultural conduct which can be called the "habitus." In this sense, several other fields should be explored because such kind of attention is not possible in a society where people have little attention to records as an evidence of activities.

Following three chapters investigate how record-keeping works in a specific social sphere. Chapter 5 analyzes how immigration records are kept in Japan. It examines who maintains those records and under what policies. It eventually shows that continuity and permanent preservation of those records face a challenge due to the official stance that "there are no immigrants" and a vertically divided administrative structure. Chapter 6 describes how the Japanese style of organization has influenced records management and information disclosure practices. It concludes that information disclosure often fails due to a tendency to avoid transparency despite the effective records management system to preserve public records in the administrative organization in Japan. Chapter 7 addresses the development of the education to be an archivist in Japan focusing on the "Standard of Tasks and Competitiveness for Archivist" by the National Archives of Japan. It points out that while the archivist education system has developed for a decade, issues of employment instability, compensation, and professional education remain. And finally, Chap. 8 is a little bit unique because it addresses the usage of number as scientific evidence in the field of environmental pollution of a religious country, Iran. In our discussion, we take the supposition of records as evidence as granted so far but what we regard as evidence is an interesting question to consider with serious attention. This chapter provides some insights about it.

We hope that this book will provide people around the world with some suggestion about the relationship between archives and a democratic society.

Ibaraki, Japan Keiji Fujiyoshi

# Acknowledgment

Our research has been supported and encouraged by a lot of colleagues, scholars and archivists inside and outside of Japan. We express a profound gratitude to those who generously provided us with their insights based on their scholarship and everyday practice.

We had an opportunity to share some of our research output with the scholars in September 2024. It was at the International Sociological Association Research Committee 25 Interim Conference held in Warsaw, Poland. There we found important and stimulating feedback. Prof. Anna Odrowaz-Coates and her Polish colleagues at The Maria Grzegorzewska University made it possible. This opportunity helped us to review our discussion before publication.

This work was supported by JSPS KAKENHI Grant Number 23K22190.

# Contents

# List of Figures

# List of Tables

# Chapter 1
# Public Scandals that Raised Awareness of the Government's Records Management

**Keiji Fujiyoshi**

**Abstract** This chapter briefly recounts four public scandals related to the Japanese government's records management in the postwar years and describes the implications of those scandals. By doing so, it explains why and how secure records management and its appropriate disclosure are important for the dependable maintenance of a democratic society properly governed by a state power. It also points out the double status of people who are subject to the state's rules, on one hand, and who are at the same time potentially capable of revising the state's rules. The chapter concludes by underlining the importance of public records as the link between the people and their government.

**Keywords** Fifty million floating pension records · Friendly authoritarianism · Checks and evaluations by the people · PKO Act · Toshio Akagi · National Strategic Special Zones · Return of Okinawa · Popular sovereignty

## 1.1 Introduction

In 2011, the International Council on Archives (ICA) proposed the Universal Declaration on Archives (UDA) to the 36th Session of the General Conference of UNESCO, and the Declaration was adopted at the Conference.[1] The Declaration includes several elements, among which one can discern an emphasis on the crucial role of archives in ensuring administrative transparency and democratic accountability. In short, the Declaration regards archives as an indispensable instrument for a democratic society.

[1] https://www.ica.org/resource/universal-declaration-on-archives-uda/

K. Fujiyoshi (✉)
Faculty of Sociology, Otemon Gakuin University, Ibaraki-shi, Osaka, Japan
e-mail: fjosh524@hotmail.com



K. Fujiyoshi (ed.), *Governance, Ignorance, and Archives*,
https://doi.org/10.1007/978-981-95-1962-0_1

We know there are many countries which have adopted democratic systems to govern their societies, but we also know that democratic systems vary from one country to another. Hence, we can agree that the importance and characteristics of archives as indispensable implements for democracy may differ somewhat from country to country.

This is why Japanese society deserves to be scrutinized closely from several vantage points to shed light on the relationship between archives and democracy. Japan has usually been regarded as a democratic state at least since the end of World War II, but the role of archives as part of the infrastructure of democratic society has been overlooked for decades in Japanese society. It would be hasty, however, to regard Japan as a democratic state without the foundation of records. Records of course play an important role in multiple social spheres of Japan, but Japanese society sometimes lacks a sense of accountability and transparency.

From this perspective, this chapter surveys how records and archives—especially those of governments—are regarded and handled, and how that influences the function or malfunction of Japan's democratic system. That will shed light on the social, cultural, and historical characteristics of the role of records in Japan and provide some insight into the relationship between the public and the government in one of the world's democratic countries. This chapter examines several public scandals that arose from the government's mishandling (intended or not) of records. Those recordkeeping-related scandals revealed how both the government and the public recognized the validity of the records held by the government, which suggests something about the relationship between records and the government in Japan.

In the first two decades of the twenty-first century, several serious scandals related to the government's recordkeeping occurred in Japan. A few significant events briefly examined here will elucidate some of the problems with the Japanese government's current recordkeeping system.

## 1.2 Fifty Million Floating Pension Records

In May 2007, the Japanese government announced that about 50 million records for social security pensions were "floating." According to Japanese pension economist Noriyuki Takayama (2009), Japan uses several social security pension schemes for different sectors of the population. The oldest scheme dates back to 1884 and has a history of more than 140 years. The newest one was established in 1961. Those schemes each issued pension identification numbers to each enrollee independently from the other schemes. Moreover, new numbers were issued to people when, for example, they moved to other regions or took employment at other companies. New pension numbers were also issued to enrollees when they acquired new family names due to marriage or divorce. As a result, many Japanese were likely to have two or more pension identification numbers issued before retirement by several programs in which they had once been enrolled.

In January 1997, the Japanese government introduced a unified pension identification number system covering all eligible persons in Japan. In the process of implementing the unified pension identification number system, the government found that there were about 50,950,000 pension records which could not have been integrated into the unified number system. These were the "floating" numbers (Japan Pension Service 2024).[2] As of 2024, the government has identified and unified 21,040,000 records, but the rest are still under investigation for several reasons.[3]

Most of the people whose floating numbers were later successfully integrated were classified into these three categories:[4]

1. They changed jobs many times before retirement. Some of their pension numbers, especially those of enrollees in the early stages of their careers, had not been identified at the time of their retirement.
2. Their family names changed due to marriage or divorce during their careers. The family name is one of the indispensable identifiers for pension records, so if enrollees got married and took their spouses' surnames, the pension records registered under their former family names sometimes were, accidentally or mistakenly, not tethered to their renewed records.
3. They had family names that have several readings, which were not correctly included in the process of insurance number unification.

The third point was crucial for the process of digital number unification at that time in a society using Chinese characters. For example, Watanabe is one of the most-used family names in Japan, and it is written with the Chinese characters 渡辺. However, 渡辺 can also be read Watabe. One cannot tell which is the proper reading for a particular person just by seeing the Chinese characters; one must be told how to read it by a person who has that name, or by others who know it. There are other factors which further complicate the matter. The name Watabe has another set of Chinese characters: 渡部, and it can also be read Watanabe. Hence, there are four possibilities among two Watanabes both in Chinese characters and in readings. To make the matter even more troublesome, there are several Chinese characters with alternate forms for 辺, such as 邊 or 邉.

Pension registration records were originally created and maintained by handwriting on paper. According to Takayama (2009), all pension records were kept in handwritten paper form prior to the introduction of digitized records in the 1960s. In the process of transferring these written records to computer records via punch cards, Japanese names written in Chinese characters could not be handled properly because of technological limitations at the time.

This means that many persons named Watanabe and Watabe could not keep their original names in Chinese characters after being transferred to the pension-related

[2] https://www.nenkin.go.jp/service/nenkinkiroku/torikumi/sonota/kini-cam/20150601-05.html

[3] https://www.nenkin.go.jp/service/nenkinkiroku/torikumi/torikumijokyo/20150501.files/00000291543ecbUY2Wvn.pdf

[4] https://www.nenkin.go.jp/service/nenkinkiroku/torikumi/sonota/kini-cam/20150601-05.files/0000009880OnzusK6XWO.pdf

digitized personal data. Needless to say, it happened not merely to Watanabes and Watabes but also to those who had similar complexity in their name, and as a result, the blunder has made it difficult or even impossible to identify who enrolled, or once had been enrolled, in which pension program during what time span.

The government of a state has a variety of tasks on multiple levels, among which ensuring safe lives and good health for its citizens should be recognized as one of the most crucial. Living a safe and healthy life without financial distress after retirement is, in this sense, one of the most important things that governments should do for their people. Of course, nobody is perfect and no government is free from making mistakes, but Japan's case was a colossal blunder that cannot be overlooked. It was not a simple human error; instead, it should be seen as an ill-conceived transition from paper-based records to digital records of pension information using the technologically restricted means of that time. Furthermore, a considerable amount of original paper records had been discarded before their information could be transferred. Individual pension records include certain pieces of information to correctly identify enrollees in the program, such as family name, given name, date of birth, place of birth, name(s) of companies where enrollees worked, retirement date, and type of pension. In October 2008, Nobuto Hosaka, then a member of House of Representatives from the opposition Social Democratic Party, addressed the 170th Diet[5] and asked about the destruction of paper pension records. He pointed out that the transfer of company names had not been done in the process of pension record migration from paper to digital media.

Actually, the Social Insurance Agency (SIA), which was the organization that managed and implemented social insurance systems in Japan, informed all eligible enrollees of their unified identification numbers in the early stage of pension number integration. The SIA sent them postcards, asking whether they had used multiple identification numbers for pensions in the past and to send their reply cards containing a list of all pension numbers they had used in the past, if any. The SIA received only 9.16 million replies (around 9%), at that time (Takayama 2009).

True, the government was not very sincere about securing the pension system for its citizens, but here we should admit that most Japanese people also were not very interested in making the government secure their pension systems. They might not have paid much attention to the fact that certain kinds of records kept by the government were crucial for, and indispensable to, their post-retirement lives. Arguably, most of them did not perceive the government as a means of keeping them safe and healthy, even though they understood that they were ruled by their government. They were not very careful about monitoring the government's performance to make sure their lives and welfare were safe and stable.

It is generally known that until the end of World War II, Japan was under the Meiji Constitution and the people were subjects of the Emperor. The people were likely to think that something provided for them by the government was a blessing from the Emperor. Such an ambience has long pervaded throughout the second half

[5] https://www.shugiin.go.jp/internet/itdb_shitsumon.nsf/html/shitsumon/a170131.htm

of the twentieth century after the unconditional surrender to the Allied Forces and the acceptance of the Potsdam Declaration in 1945, which is described as "friendly authoritarianism" by Sugimito (2010). Any kind of service was often regarded as the "mercy" of the government, which of course rejected checks and evaluations by the people. This point shall be discussed in the following sections.

## 1.3 Missing Troop Logs of GSDF in Iraq

The Self-Defense Forces (SDF) of Japan were established in 1954, 9 years after Japan's surrender in World War II and the year after the Korean War ended. The creation of the SDF has been the subject of fierce domestic controversy for decades. Japanese people at that time were still sick of their previous war experience and had a deep-rooted dislike of the belligerent intentions that the Japanese government shared with the United States as one of the Western democratic countries in the early stage of the Cold War. The Constitution of Japan, which took effect in 1947, was a comprehensive revision of the Meiji Constitution that had administered the Japanese political apparatus for more than 80 years until the end of World War II. In contrast to the Meiji Constitution, the new Constitution aimed to maintain and develop Japan as a democratic and peaceful state. It confirms three principles: popular sovereignty, respect for fundamental human rights, and pacifism.[6] Among them, the third was earnestly welcomed by Japanese people who had survived the American air raids that had burned over 60 major cities, including Tokyo and Osaka, and killed over 400,000 civilians from 1944 to 1945.[7] This pacifism or war-weariness has commonly been connected with the renunciation of war and restraint over the possession of armed forces. This is why the SDF have been a very sensitive and controversial subject that has aroused heated debates many times inside and outside of the National Diet.

Under these circumstances, postwar Japan certainly behaved as part of the Western liberal bloc during the Cold War, but it was also very careful to keep itself a pacifist state owing to concerns about the citizens' aversion to war, as well as the suspicions of neighboring countries about Japan's intention to rearm. That is why the Japanese military forces were named the "Self-Defense Forces" and were intended to operate under a strict "exclusively defense-oriented policy."[8] Additionally, this meant that deploying SDF forces abroad was long out of the question for any reason.

In 1992, a year after the Gulf War was triggered by the Iraqi invasion and occupation of Kuwait, the International Peace Cooperation Act (PKO Act) was enacted

---

[6] Prime Minister of Japan and His Cabinet. https://japan.kantei.go.jp/constitution_and_government_of_japan/constitution_e.html

[7] NHK Archives. https://www2.nhk.or.jp/archives/articles/?id=C0060015

[8] Ministry of Defense. https://www.mod.go.jp/en/d_policy/basis/others/index.html

following a series of vociferous discussions.[9] Dispatching troops abroad was finally legalized under the condition that it was part of the peacekeeping operation organized by the United Nations in the region where those involved in the conflict had agreed on the ceasefire.[10] The government of Japan was then nervously cautious not to deploy the troops on the battlefield, which would conflict with the PKO Act as well as with Japan's Constitution. In order to secure the conditions for deployment, five principles for participation in the UN PKO activities had been established (gist):[11]

1. Confirmed agreement of ceasefire among those involved in the conflict;
2. Confirmed acceptance, by those involved in the conflict, of the UN Peacekeeping Force including the Japanese troops in the region of the conflict;
3. Confirmed impartiality and neutrality of the UN Peacekeeping Force;
4. Confirmed arbitrariness of the Japanese force on withdrawal from the region in case any of the above three principles is threatened; and
5. Minimal usage of arms to protect the lives and safety of the troops and personnel.

The first mission was in Angola, where one civilian and two civil servants were sent as election observers in 1992. The second was in Cambodia, where 600 troops were sent to support the United Nations Transitional Authority in Cambodia (UNTAC), together with about 70 civilian police officers and about 40 civilians. Since the first mission in Angola, troops and personnel have been dispatched to more than 10 regions. All activities in each region are supposed to be recorded to prove that they are lawfully run by their respective missions.

A scandal involving missing troop logs of the Ground Self-Defense Force (GSDF) in Iraq surfaced in 2018. It jolted not only the government but also affected the scheme of troop deployment abroad as authorized by the PKO Act, and it fomented a severe dispute over principle 1 above. There was no routine disclosure of records produced by SDF missions during the peacekeeping operations abroad, and the SDF seemed to be keeping them out of public view—and out of sight of Diet members as well.

Those events began in relation to thc logs of a mission deployed to South Sudan from January 2012 to May 2017.[12] *The Japan Times* reports in an article dated February 7, 2017:[13]

> The Defense Ministry said Tuesday it has found daily activity logs of Japanese troops in South Sudan for last July when the security situation there sharply deteriorated during U.N. peacekeeping operations, reversing its earlier position that the documents had been entirely discarded.

---

[9] Cabinet Office. https://www.cao.go.jp/pko/pko_j/info/other/other_data04.html

[10] Ministry of Foreign Affairs. https://www.mofa.go.jp/mofaj/gaiko/pko/q_a.html

[11] Ministry of Defense. https://www.mod.go.jp/j/approach/kokusai_heiwa/common/pdf/law_pko.pdf

[12] South Sudan PKO (UNMISS). https://www.mod.go.jp/en/d_act/kokusai_heiwa/pko/s_sudan_pko/index.html

[13] https://www.japantimes.co.jp/news/2017/02/07/national/politics-diplomacy/government-says-found-lost-activity-logs-gsdf-troops-south-sudan/

The Defense Ministry said "it has found" the logs. By this statement, it can be assumed that those logs had not been shared even with the Defense Ministry—which supposedly should govern the activities of Japanese PKO missions abroad—not to mention the public, as well as Diet members. Actually, the logs had been preserved by the Joint Staff Office, and their information had not been shared even with the Minister of Defense. But the scandal was just getting started. The ceasefire had been broken and the battle resumed with gunfire when the Japanese government decided to withdraw the mission from South Sudan. Some journalists or politicians directed their attention to PKO activities deployed in other regions of the world, especially in Iraq from December 2003 to February 2009. Sebata (2019) summarizes the events in the timeline as follows (excerpt):

2017

February 7

> The Ministry of Defense first answered a Japanese journalist's request for information showing that the PKO activities log in South Sudan had already been destroyed, but the ministry later retracted the answer and admitted that the log had been saved by the Joint Staff Office.

February 16

> Diet members from opposition parties asked the MoD for the activities record in Iraq, but the ministry replied that they had no related records.

February 20

> Defense Minister Tomomi Inada responded to questioning in the Diet, saying that the MoD had confirmed that it had no PKO activities records on Iraq.

March 17

> A special investigation of the South Sudan activities log commenced inside the MoD.

March 30

> The activities log on Iraq was found, but it was not regarded as a public record by the MoD because it was saved in digital format by a subdivision of MoD, which responded to the information disclosure request by saying that there was no official record about activities in Iraq.

July

> In a first for the MoD, a unified records management system was established for the PKO activity records abroad.

2018

End of February

The fact that the activities log on Iraq did exist had been shared among MoD bureaucrats.

March 31

MoD bureaucrats reported to Defense Minister Itsunori Onodera that the Iraq log had been found in January.

April 2

Onodera ordered his bureaucrats to conduct another investigation of the Iraq activities log because he was suspicious of his staff's report that the log had been found in January.

April 4

Onodera publicly announced that the log had in fact been found in March 2017.

April 16

The MoD disclosed the activities log.

Sebata (2019) also points out some problems which were revealed in the process of the above investigation.

1. Bureaucrats who conducted the investigation into the Ground Self-Defense Force knew that they had the activities log on Iraq but did not think it was a public record to be disclosed because it was a copy in digital format.
2. Most of the activity's logs created and sent to the MoD by missions deployed abroad are missing, with few exceptions such as those of South Sudan and Iraq. The logs are essential evidence about what the missions did in the regions where they were deployed, and how activities were performed. To ensure the accountability of a mission's activity, the Defense Minister could not have been too careful to safely collect and preserve those logs. It is clear that those ministers paid little attention to the matter.
3. According to a high-level SDF officer, logs were usually created and sent directly to the MoD on a daily basis by mission personnel, without any review by senior officers. This means that the MoD could not correctly or comprehensively grasp what was going on in the region where missions were deployed.
4. Both the MoD and the SDF apparently had a customary practice in which staff members used to make copies of their original records or documents, and save them when necessary for their work, then discard the originals after duplication. As a result, each member had necessary records and documents at hand, but the organization lacked integrated and systematic record keeping.
5. In relation to problem 4 above, the practice of public records classification was ruined to an unrecoverable extent. Every staff member had records and docu-

ments necessary for their jobs, but those records were usually regarded as "personal material," not as public records. Hence, the record registration system did not work, and consequently integrated and systematic intelligence activities as an organization of the MoD or SDF were made deficient or even impossible.

The last point was seen in a report by *The Mainichi Shimbun*, one of Japan's major national daily newspapers.[14] The issue was not just about whether the activities conducted by every PKO mission were lawful or not. The five principles for participation in the UN PKO activities mentioned above strictly limited the area of operations by the Japanese mission that was sent there lightly armed, and those principles urged the immediate withdrawal of missions in case there is a recurrence of armed conflict. The safety and lives of troops were at stake there.

On April 17, 2018 opposition party member Hiroe Makiyama was addressing questions to the government in the House of Councilors Committee on Foreign Affairs and Defense. She noted that, in eight locations of the disclosed log, passages had been found which included the word "battle" in the description of activities in and around Samawah.[15] Defense Minister Itsunori Onodera insisted in his answer that the word "battle" did not refer to a battle of the type in which the law prohibited participation by the Japanese mission.

Michael Bosack writes in his article about the scandal for *Tokyo Review*:[16]

> There are four layers to the log scandals: (1) handling of documents; (2) whether or not Self-Defense Force (SDF) operations violated Japan's legal frameworks; (3) civilian control of the military; and (4) civil-military relations.

This chapter's focus is on the first two layers. The SDF should conduct its behavior in accordance with the designated laws, and whether it did should be evaluated on the basis of the record, that is, the log to which this chapter has directed its attention so far. The mission must produce its everyday log neatly and correctly so that when close scrutiny is called for in the future, it can show that its activities are organized lawfully. This could be seen as the importance of the record from the viewpoint of accountability. Neither the MoD nor the SDF have paid careful and sufficient attention to this aspect of their records.

Also, their handling, or rather, mishandling, of records creates another problem for organizations. Daily logs are indispensable for missions abroad or for their headquarters in Japan to develop future plans. According to the above-mentioned high-level SDF officer, the logs sent by the deployed mission were not given appropriate attention as basic information for plan development, not only by the mission itself but also by the government. It could be said that log production was not conducted for any concrete or practical purpose.

---

[14] https://mainichi.jp/english/articles/20180406/p2a/00m/0na/013000c

[15] https://kokkai.ndl.go.jp/#/detail?minId=119613950X01120180417&spkNum=29&current=375

[16] https://www.tokyoreview.net/2018/05/self-defense-force-log-scandals/

Hence, the PKO mission produced its activities log for a hollow purpose, and that log was never appreciated as important data for the government or for the mission itself.

## 1.4 Moritomo Gakuen Scandal

Moritomo Gakuen was a private educational corporation. It was established in Osaka in the early 1970s and operated a kindergarten for more than five decades until its closure in 2021. This scandal focused public attention on the nepotism of a politician then holding public office, namely, Prime Minister Shinzo Abe, and also on the systematic falsification of government records in his favor.

The *Asahi Shimbun*, another one of Japan's major daily newspapers, reported on February 9, 2017 that the Kinki Local Finance Bureau, a regional branch of the Ministry of Finance, had sold state-owned land in Osaka to a private educational corporation for a secret amount. An investigation by the *Asahi* revealed that the price was almost one-tenth of the going price for that neighborhood.[17] The report includes the following description, although the quoted homepage of Moritomo Gakuen mentioned in the article has already been deleted from the internet.

> Moritomo Gakuen are preparing to open an elementary school in spring on the land which it purchased from the government. Mr. Kagoike, chairperson of the board of directors of the corporation, is also a board member of the Osaka branch of the Japan Conference, an organization which aims to amend the Constitution of Japan. According to the homepage of Moritomo Gakuen, the elementary school is "the first and only elementary school based on Shinto teaching," advocates "education to instill the highest regard for Japanese courtesy, and cultivates patriotism and pride as a Japanese" in its educational philosophy. The school's honorary principal is Akie Abe, wife of Prime Minister Shinzo Abe.

This report was followed by sharp criticism and disputes in the Diet over the influence of the prime minister and his wife on the disposal of a national asset to a private school at an unprecedentedly low price. In his answer to a question by a member of the Diet from an opposition party on February 17, Prime Minister Abe resolutely denied the accusation and confirmed that he would resign his post as Prime Minister as well as a Member of the Diet if the accusation were proved.[18] Nobuhisa Sagawa, a senior MoF official, answered the question of a Diet member, saying that the deal had been conducted lawfully and that there had been no intervention or pressure from any politicians about it. Sagawa responded to the request to disclose the records of negotiations with Moritomo, saying that such documents were preserved for a very short term, usually shorter than 1 year, and that most of them had been discarded.

---

[17] https://www.asahi.com/articles/ASK264H4YK26PPTB00J.html

[18] https://www.shugiin.go.jp/internet/itdb_kaigiroku.nsf/html/kaigiroku/001819320170217012.htm

Despite the incandescent language, the opposition party members' pursuit lacked decisive force. One of the reasons for this misfired pursuit seemed to be that they lacked knowledge about what kind of records were created and how long they were preserved in the ministries. To put it more succinctly, the government's record retention schedule had not been shared with Diet members or even with the public.

The Diet session ended in June of that year without any significant result about the scandal. There was a House of Representatives election the following October, in which the ruling Liberal Democratic Party won 284 of 465 seats. The coalition government headed by Shinzo Abe thereby secured the support of the 284 LDP seats, combined with 29 Komeito seats. Apparently, the scandal had had little impact on the Abe Cabinet.

On March 2, 2018, about 1 year after the first report, the *Asahi Shimbun* again published a report alleging that government records had been falsified after its first report.[19] In a follow-up report 1 week later, it revealed that the record of finalized approval had been falsified. For example, certain phrases such as "the exceptionality of this case," which hinted at the involvement of the prime minister, had been excised from the finalized document at the time of the contract. The report also said that a page of text crucial to the contract had been deleted or altered. On the same day, Nobuhisa Sagawa resigned as commissioner of the National Tax Agency. The stated reason was that he shouldered the relevant responsibility in MoF when the Moritomo-related government documents were submitted to the Diet. In short, he was regarded as responsible for the falsification of the documents.

On March 12, Minister of Finance Taro Aso issued a comment admitting that the MoF had falsified 14 items which involved deleting the names of politicians and the prime minister's wife, along with phrases such as "the exceptionality of this case."[20]

It was eventually confirmed that falsification of the relevant government records was an initiative of MoF senior official Nobuhisa Sagawa.

On March 7, which fell between the *Asahi*'s report and MoF's admission, a person named Toshio Akagi took his life at home. He was 54 years old then. He had been working for the Kinki Local Finance Bureau, a regional MoF branch, and he admitted in writing that he had falsified the Moritomo-related records under an order of the ministry on February 26, 2017. He had been diagnosed with depression several months before his death.[21]

Akagi's wife Masako published the daily memoranda and final note of her late husband on March 18, 2020, 2 years after his death. On the same day, she filed a lawsuit against Nobuhisa Sagawa and the MoF demanding disclosure of all documents related to the Moritomo scandal, which she believed had driven her husband to suicide. In her lawsuit, she also demanded compensation of 5.5 million yen. Even though the government had already admitted its responsibility for Akagi's death, the Supreme Court dismissed her suit against Sagawa on the grounds that there is

[19] https://www.asahi.com/articles/ASLD63VMCLD6PTIL00V.html

[20] https://www.mof.go.jp/public_relations/statement/other/search_kessaibunsho.htm

[21] https://www.asahi.com/articles/ASN7H56V4N7GPTIL02T.html

already a judicial precedent which exempts public servants from liability for compensation covering any damage caused by conduct in the course of duty.[22] The lawsuit did not result in a satisfactory judgment for the plaintiff, but some related records have been released by the government little by little since then.[23]

While the Moritomo scandal was being subjected to scrutiny in the Diet, another scandal erupted over the approval process for establishing a new faculty at a university. In 1966, Kitazato University won approval to establish a Department of Veterinary Medicine in the Faculty of Animal Science. Since then, the Ministry of Education, Culture, Sports, Science, and Technology (MEXT, formerly the Ministry of Education) has upheld its policy of restricting the establishment of more of the same faculty at Japanese universities while paying close attention to the nationwide supply-and-demand balance of veterinarians. According to a report by Japanese public broadcaster NHK,[24] this change was made in 2013 when the National Strategic Special Zone System was created. In 2016, the Council on National Strategic Special Zones, chaired by Prime Minister Shinzo Abe, designated Imabari City on Shikoku Island as one of the National Strategic Special Zones and allowed it to establish faculties of veterinary medicine despite the long restriction on doing so.

The approval conditions were unreasonably strict:

1. On January 4, 2017, the Cabinet Office called for a proposal to establish a faculty of veterinary medicine in Imabari City, the location which had already been chosen. Another candidate for the faculty was Kyoto City, but it was excluded from consideration without any explicit or rational reasons.
2. The applicant would have to start operation of the faculty in April 2018, just 1 year after the call.
3. Only one university was approved for the establishment of such a faculty in Japan.
4. The application period was 8 days.

There was only one applicant for the call and that was Kake Gakuen (Kake Educational Institution). The *Mainichi* reports it as follows:[25]

> Following the Moritomo case, another favoritism scandal involving Abe surfaced in connection with a veterinarian school that opened in the Ehime Prefecture city of Imabari in April 2018 as part of the Okayama University of Science. The school is operated by Kake Educational Institution, which is based in the western Japan city of Okayama. Kotaro Kake, chairman of the university operator, is Abe's close friend. Documents supposedly containing accounts from the prime minister's secretary, in which the secretary called the establishment of the vet school a "matter concerning the prime minister," and from Abe himself, in

[22] https://www3.nhk.or.jp/kansai-news/20250314/2000092427.html

[23] https://mainichi.jp/english/articles/20210913/p2a/00m/0na/026000c

[24] https://web.archive.org/web/20170525234122/http://www3.nhk.or.jp/news/html/20170525/k10010995051000.html

[25] https://mainichi.jp/english/articles/20200829/p2a/00m/0na/020000c

which he apparently told Kake that opening a new vet school was "a good idea," remain at the Ehime Prefectural Government.

On November 15, MEXT Minister Yoshimasa Hayashi announced the ministry's acknowledgment, with the understanding that the approval procedure had been done lawfully.

Being close friends is not a reason for an accusation of fraud, although it leaves room for suspicion. Two people might be comrades who pursue the same ideal together, but it is not illegal to be friends with a shared aim. What was necessary here was a fair procedure for approval and the official record to prove the procedure was conducted on the basis of appropriate criteria and proper procedure. Public attention seemed to be focused on the closeness of the prime minister and the school operator, but what should have been scrutinized was whether the project deserved approval to be granted a huge chunk of the national budget. The question has never been sufficiently answered.

## 1.5 Secret Agreement: Ministry of Foreign Affairs Secret Leak Incident

This chapter has so far explored three public scandals regarding the records management of governmental bodies in Japan early in the twenty-first century. Comprehensively exploring the system of records management and archives in Japan is impossible in this short chapter but it provides some insight into the relationship of the Japanese public and public records. There have been many scandals involving politicians in modern Japan, as is often the case in other countries. People get angry when a scandal is revealed, as is often the case as well. Subsequently, however, their anger soon vaporizes as usual, at least in Japan. People are so busy making ends meet that they lack the time to constantly watch what their government does, and how. That is why public records are important. With the help of such records, people are able to observe what the government has done, and journalists do so on behalf of the people. In this sense, public records are an indispensable means for checking the conduct of the government, which in turn is an indispensable means of keeping the people's lives safe and comfortable. At any rate, people can see both the government and public records as valuable tools for their own welfare, which are funded by their own taxes.

How to use public and government records is, therefore, closely connected with how to use the government. Public records will be just a weapon to attack and damage the government as a public asset unless people recognize it as their own. This section examines a record-related scandal from about a half century ago.

After World War II, Japan was occupied by Allied Forces headed by American General Douglas MacArthur. The occupation ended in 1951 with the signing of the Treaty of San Francisco, also called the Treaty of Peace with Japan. But even after the treaty came into force in 1952, some former Japanese territories had still not been returned to Japan, instead remaining under US rule. One of these territories was the Okinawa Islands, also called the Ryukyu Islands.

In 1965, then Prime Minister Eisaku Sato visited Okinawa, which was the first visit to the islands by a Japanese prime minister after World War II. He stated that Japan's postwar status would not be over until Okinawa was returned to the motherland,[26] and he showed his strong willingness to make it happen. Nine years after that, he was awarded the Nobel Peace Prize "for his contribution to stabilize conditions in the Pacific rim area and for signing the Nuclear Non-Proliferation Treaty" in 1974.[27]

The process of returning Okinawa to Japan was not easy, as returning occupied land is usually a difficult matter. It is really true when a defeated country is to retrieve its lost land from the country that defeated it. After his visit in 1965, Sato made efforts to negotiate with the United States on the issue of returning Okinawa, which was already regarded as the "Keystone of the Pacific" 12 years after the end of the Korean War and just after the beginning of US President Lyndon Johnson's bombing campaign of North Vietnam. It was the Cold War era, and that was when the Ministry of Foreign Affairs' Secret Leak Incident occurred.

In 1969, Prime Minister Sato visited President Richard Nixon in Washington to exchange views on the contemporary international situation and on other matters of common interest to the United States and Japan. After their talk, they issued a joint statement which included an agreement that the reversion of Okinawa should be completed by 1972 at the latest.[28]

It was just 20 years after the end of World War II when Sato visited Okinawa. Memories of the battle, arbitrary and frequent strafing from the air, and heavy bombardment from naval gunfire were still fresh in the minds of, and traumatic for, the people in Okinawa. Additionally, most of their farmland had been devastated by some 3 months of bombardment, and daily necessities including food were lacking. Every day was a struggle to survive. Okinawans of course were eager to recover their Japanese nationality after American rule, but they also faced the desperate need of compensation for hardship under conditions of the occupation. Questions in this context were: whether Okinawa would be returned to Japan free of nuclear weapons; how much of the land being used by the US Army would be returned to Japanese civilians, most of whom were farmers; whether the returned land would be restored as farmland or remain as base facilities; and whether the United States would grant compensation for the loss of farmland.

The return of Okinawa was of interest not only to the Okinawan people and to politicians like Sato, because it also held the attention of the Japanese public and journalists. Newspapers presented topics such as when Okinawa would be returned,

---

[26] National Archives of Japan, Return of Okinawa. https://www.archives.go.jp/exhibition/digital/high-growth/contents/23/index.html

[27] Nobel Prize Foundation. https://www.nobelprize.org/prizes/peace/1974/sato/facts/

[28] The American Presidency Project. https://www.presidency.ucsb.edu/documents/joint-statement-following-discussions-with-prime-minister-sato-japan

how it would be accomplished, and how much it would cost. Public attention focused on these questions even 20 years after the end of World War II.

On June 17, 1971, after several years of preliminary negotiations, the Okinawa Reversion Agreement was signed by both the United States and Japan. It was ratified on November 24 by the Diet and then enacted on May 15 of the following year. The document featured eight points agreed upon by the two parties, which shows that the details of the agreement had not been shared with the public or even with Diet members in Japan when the agreement was signed by the two countries. Opposition parties and journalists were eager to make the government admit the agreement had several uncertain points to be confirmed before ratification by the Diet.

One of the key issues was the expense of relocation and removal of American facilities and properties (Sawachi 2006). The US government had already confirmed to Congress that reversion would require no expenditure by the United States. On the contrary, the Japanese government had proposed that the United States pay a restoration compensation fee. In the process of negotiation, the Japanese government could find no room for concessions on the US side, so the government eventually decided to include the fee in the cost of relocation and removal of American facilities and properties, which the two governments had agreed would be shouldered by Japan. The Japanese government floated a proposal in the Diet for the total expense that Japan would have to pay for the reversion of Okinawa, but would not reveal the specifics. Sawachi (2006) explains the procedure as follows:

> The United States accepted Japan's claim for restoration compensation, which is made possible by the "Disposition of trust funds received from foreign governments for citizens of United States," enacted in February 1896.[29] Acceptance is possible only if (1) Japan says that the compensation fee shall be no more than 4 million US dollars; (2) the Japanese foreign minister sends a note promising that the Japanese government will give the United States government 4 million US dollars so that it will be able to establish a trust fund to compensate Japan for the restoration of land in Okinawa; (3) The note shall be kept top secret; and (4) The Japanese proposal shall be declined unless the note is produced. In this way, Japan assumed the compensation responsibility of the United States and gave the Japanese public the impression that the US would pay.

This is how the secret agreement was concluded. Among the eight points of the agreement,[30] there was a reference to expenditure in Article VII, which reads:

> Article VII
>
> Considering inter alia that United States assets are being transferred to the Government of Japan under Article VI of this Agreement, that the Government of the United States of America is carrying out the return of the Ryukyu Islands and the Daito Islands to Japan in a manner consistent with the policy of the Government of Japan as specified in paragraph 8 of the Joint Communique of November 21,1969, and that the Government of the United States of America will bear extra costs, particularly in the area of employment after rever-

[29] https://www.law.cornell.edu/uscode/text/22/2668a

[30] https://www.nytimes.com/1971/06/18/archives/text-of-usjapanese-treaty-restoringokinawa-and-nearby-islands-to.html, and then add The New York Times, Text of U.S.-Japanese Treaty Restoring Okinawa and Nearby Islands to Tokyo, into News Outlets (in English).

sion, the Government of Japan will pay to the Government of the United States of America in United States dollars a total amount of three hundred and twenty million United States dollars (U. S. $320,000,000) over a period of five years from the date of entry into force of this Agreement. Of the said amount, the Government of Japan will pay one hundred million United States dollars (U. S. $100,000,000) within one week after the date of entry into force of this Agreement and the remainder in four equal annual installments in June of each calendar year subsequent to the year in which this Agreement enters into force.

There are two passages referring to payment:

1. the Government of the United States of America will bear extra costs, particularly in the area of employment after reversion;
2. the Government of Japan will pay to the Government of the United States of America in United States dollars a total amount of 320 million United States dollars (U. S. $320,000,000).

In the Diet, the opposition parties were eager to get an answer from the government about how much the Government of the United States would pay, and about the breakdown of Japanese expenditures of US$320 million. They were skeptical about the expenditures of the United States and therefore they assumed that the amount of subrogation would be included in the Japanese expenditures.

In short, their assumption was right but their pursuit of the information was not so successful. Outside the Diet, some of the secret telegrams of the Japanese government concerning the subrogation were being leaked to a Japanese journalist by an MoFA staff member. The journalist, Takichi Nishiyama, was a *Mainichi Shimbun* reporter whose beat was the MoFA at that time. Most ministries provide a room in their buildings for journalists working at approved major news outlets such as newspapers, magazines, and broadcasters. Those rooms are called "Reporters' Club" or similar names. The permitted journalists are usually stationed in those rooms and visit the officials, sometimes high-ranking, who work in the same building to get information of public interest. Having a place in a ministry building is a kind of privilege granted to the reporters of major media, and they get personally acquainted with those officials. Such relationships become more than business in several ways.

In the early spring of 1971, the *Mainichi* assigned Nishiyama to the MoFA, which was the second time in his career. He had many acquaintances and even friends in the ministry; he also had some expertise in the foreign affairs of Japan. The *Mainichi* expected that he would do well as a leader of the foreign affairs reporting team of the paper in the final stage of negotiations between Japan and the United States over the reversion of Okinawa.

At the Foreign Ministry Nishiyama got acquainted, and then intimate, with a female official of the ministry. With her assistance, Nishiyama covertly obtained secret telegrams concerning the reversion of Okinawa several times. This could be seen as an act of newsgathering based on an affair. The telegrams were not published by the *Mainichi*, but were handed to some opposition-party Diet members. After receiving the documents from Nishiyama, the opposition-party Diet members persistently quizzed the government about the subrogation, insinuating that they already had those secret telegrams in their possession. As a result, opposition party members showed the duplicated telegrams to Foreign Ministry officials as evidence of government cheating, which revealed how the secret had been leaked. Officials soon identified the "deep throat" in the organization, and the government counterattacked immediately. That shifted the public's attention to the misconduct of the *Mainichi* reporter and the breach of confidentiality by the female official who was acting as a public servant. Success by the efforts of Foreign Ministry officials led to the arrests of both Nishiyama and his paramour, who were subsequently found guilty in court. Meanwhile, the Okinawa Reversion Agreement was ratified by the National Diet on November 24, 1971 (Sawachi 2006).

The *Mainichi* issued a statement saying that the arrest of the reporter was an unacceptable threat to the public's right to know, but the statement did not have the intended effect of diverting the public's attention from the affair of a newspaper reporter and a government official. The scandal showed that the government's operations were not secure enough to keep its crucial information secret, a situation that might have given the United States an advantage over Japan in the final stage of negotiations.

## 1.6 Conclusion: Records as a Tool of Governance

Records as a tool of governance are usually considered from a ruler's viewpoint (Ketelaar 2005). State power collects and keeps the population's information in order to efficiently control and tax them. This is the case for almost all state powers, although to what extent it does so differs from one country to another. In this sense, most people think of themselves as the ruled, or to say it more politely, as the governed. No matter whether the state is democratic or authoritarian, its people should generally be subject to the state's rule. On this point as well, there is no difference regarding whether the state is democratic or authoritarian. Then what does a state being democratic imply?

Karel van Wolferen is a Dutch journalist who was stationed in Japan as a Far East correspondent when in 1994 he wrote the book *The False Realities of a Politicized Society*, which was originally published in Japanese. In his discussion on the relationship between democracy and bureaucracy, he writes, "The problem to carefully think over is how the system to control the bureaucrats can be established given that their fundamental mission is to control the public" (Wolferen 1994). The statement is still valid 30 years after he made the observation. People should be subjects that the state rules, but, on the other hand, they are, to some extent, able to choose and decide what rules they want to obey. Roughly speaking, they strive to attain the rules they prefer to follow, but they should follow the current rules. Democracy based on popular sovereignty assumes that state leaders should be chosen by the people. Collins online dictionary defines the general meaning of popular sovereignty as follows :[31]

---

[31] https://www.collinsdictionary.com/dictionary/english/popular-sovereignty

> the doctrine that sovereign power is vested in the people and that those chosen to govern, as trustees of such power, must exercise it in conformity with the general will

People choose the state leaders but they don't allow their leaders a free hand. Those leaders should rule in compliance with the existing rules, and the rules can be modified by the representatives the people choose in elections. This is a very simplified description of how the government functions in a democratic society.

Japan had a history of more than 300 years of authoritarian society before it established the Meiji Constitution, and the Meiji state too was authoritarian. That sometimes affects the people's attitude toward state power. For example, Japan has a universal health insurance system.[32] Some may see it as a favor of the ruler, but it is not. The National Health Insurance Act was enacted in 1958. It was approved in the Diet by the representatives of the Japanese people, and its universality is limited by the nation's international border. The Japanese people approved the system via their elected lawmakers. They entrusted their government with the implementation of the system to safeguard people's health. This requires dependable records' management and disclosure. The government must use the proof afforded by appropriately collected and classified records to show the citizens that its work is reliable. The citizens can thereby see the soundness of their government's work on the basis of its business records. Records have the indispensable role of linkage between popular sovereignty and the government.

People are subject to the law so that it will secure their safety and comfort, and in some cases, even help them live worthwhile lives, as well as giving them a sense of exhilaration at the prospects of future developments, such as legalizing same-sex marriage or different surnames for married couples. That is to say, people are always in the process of revising and improving the laws which control and better their lives.

We all play our own parts in the world. Where and under what rules to play had already been decided when we made our appearance here. We respect the rules if we think they provide comfort and are reasonable to follow at the time.

It may be good for us here to recall an ordeal suffered in 1983 by Diego Maradona, the legendary Argentinian soccer player. The forward player of FC Barcelona was violently tackled by an Athletic Club defender in a match with La Liga, the Spanish Football League, and his left ankle was broken. There arose much impassioned and vigorous dispute over the incident,[33] but what we should recall here is that the fans and supporters, as well as players themselves, thought that they loved games, hard plays, and of course victories, but that they did not want their adored and extraordinary players to hurt one another with unfair conduct on the pitch. The game rules have since been revised to strictly prohibit dangerous plays.

This can be adapted to a society and state. People live their own lives in accordance with the established laws of society, but at the same time, they are capable of revising and modifying those laws in accordance with their expected reasonableness. Of course, the reality is not as easy as this simple explanation, but the Japanese

---

[32] https://www.mhlw.go.jp/english/org/policy/p34-35.html

[33] https://www.marca.com/en/football/barcelona/2018/09/24/5ba90cb522601d0e698b463d.html

people have five decades of the experience relating to public records, and that experience shows how important the role of records and archives is for the people to observe and control the government which controls them.

**Acknowledgement** This work was supported by JSPS KAKENHI Grant Number 23K22190.

## References[34]

### *Books and Articles*

Ketelaar E (2005) Recordkeeping and societal power. In: Mckemmish S et al (eds) Archives: recordkeeping in society. Centre for Information Studies

Sawachi H (2006) Mitsuyaku (secret agreement). Iwanami Shoten [AZ-717-H14]

Sebata H (2019) Kokka to Kiroku (state and records). Shueisha [AZ-311-M35]

Sugimito Y (2010) An introduction to Japanese Society, 3rd edn. Cambridge UP

Takayama N (2009) On fifty million floating pension records in Japan. In: Geneva papers on risk and insurance-issues and practice 34. https://www.ier.hit-u.ac.jp/pie/stage2/English/report/PR0906/3.1%20takayama.pdf

Wolferen K (1994) Ningen wo koufuku ni sinai nihon toiu shisutemu. English edition: The false realities of a politicized society. Mainichi Shimbun sha [GB63-E74]

### *News Outlets (in English)*

### *Japan Times*

Government says it has 'found' lost activity logs of GSDF troops in South Sudan, The Japan Times, February 7, 2017. https://www.japantimes.co.jp/news/2017/02/07/national/politics-diplomacy/government-says-found-lost-activity-logs-gsdf-troops-south-sudan/

### *Mainichi*

Critics slam Japan PM Abe for dodging accountability over scandals with exit decision, The Mainichi. August 29, 2020. https://mainichi.jp/english/articles/20200829/p2a/00m/0na/020000c

Deceased Japan bureaucrat left copy of email seen as start of doc tampering scandal. The Mainichi, September 14, 2021. https://mainichi.jp/english/articles/20210913/p2a/00m/0na/026000c

GSDF section chief didn't report Iraq logs as he didn't think they were disputed in Diet, The Mainichi, April 6, 2018. https://mainichi.jp/english/articles/20180406/p2a/00m/0na/013000c

[34] Given in brackets (ex. [EG283-372]) are the National Diet Library Call Numbers, which provide Japanese bibliographic information. https://iss.ndl.go.jp/.

Note: All webpages were accessed on April 3, 2025.

## Marca

Goikoetxea's challenge on Maradona that left a lasting impression on Spanish football, Marca, September 24, 2018. https://www.marca.com/en/football/barcelona/2018/09/24/5ba90cb522601d0e698b463d.html

## Tokyo Review

What to make of the Self-Defense Force 'Log Scandals' by Michael Bosack. Tokyo Review, May 30, 2018. https://www.tokyoreview.net/2018/05/self-defense-force-log-scandals/

## News Outlets (in Japanese)

## Asahi Shimbun

Gakkouhoujin ni Osaka no kokuyuuchi baikyaku, kakaku hikouhyou, kinrin no ichiwari ka (Disposal by sale of the state-owned land to a private school corporation, price not revealed, one-tenth that of nearby land?). Asahi Shimbun, February 9, 2017. https://www.asahi.com/articles/ASK264H4YK26PPTB00J.html

Moritomo mondai wa owatte inai, jikeiretsu de furikaeru ichiren no keii (Moritomo scandal not over, series of events in timeline). Asahi Shimbun, December 19, 2018. https://www.asahi.com/articles/ASLD63VMCLD6PTIL00V.html

Otto no saigo no kao wa zetsubou ni michite ita, Akagi san tsuma no chinnjutsu zenbun (When I last saw my husband's face it was full of despair, full statement of Akagi's wife). Asahi Shimbun, July 15, 2020). https://www.asahi.com/articles/ASN7H56V4N7GPTIL02T.html

## NHK

'Kake Gakuen' juui gakubu shinsetsu mondai 4 tsu no ronten ('Kake Gakuen': Four points regarding the establishment of a new veterinary school, NHK, May 25, 2017, retrieved via Wayback Machine). https://web.archive.org/web/20170525234122/http://www3.nhk.or.jp/news/html/20170525/k10010995051000.html

Moritomo bunsho, zaimu shou moto kyokuchou no baishou sekinin mitomenai hanketsu kakutei, saikousai (Moritomo document: ruling denying the former Finance Ministry director's liability for damages finalized). NHK, March 14, 2025). https://www3.nhk.or.jp/kansai-news/20250314/2000092427.html

## Resources on the Web (in English)

Collins Dictionary (popular sovereignty). https://www.collinsdictionary.com/dictionary/english/popular-sovereignty

Cornell Law School, 22 U.S. Code § 2668a - Disposition of trust funds received from foreign governments for citizens of United States. https://www.law.cornell.edu/uscode/text/22/2668a

International Council on Archives, The Universal Declaration on Archives. https://www.ica.org/resource/universal-declaration-on-archives-uda/

Ministry of Defense, Other Basic Policies. https://www.mod.go.jp/en/d_policy/basis/others/index.html
Ministry of Defense, South Sudan PKO (UNMISS). https://www.mod.go.jp/en/d_act/kokusai_heiwa/pko/s_sudan_pko/index.html
Ministry of Health, Labour and Welfare, Health Insurance Bureau. https://www.mhlw.go.jp/english/org/policy/p34-35.html
Nobel Prize Foundation, Eisaku Sato. https://www.nobelprize.org/prizes/peace/1974/sato/facts/
Prime Minister of Japan and His Cabinet, The Constitution of Japan. https://japan.kantei.go.jp/constitution_and_government_of_japan/constitution_e.html
The American Presidency Project, Nixon R: Joint Statement Following Discussions With Prime Minister Sato of Japan. https://www.presidency.ucsb.edu/documents/joint-statement-following-discussions-with-prime-minister-sato-japan

## *Resources on the Web (in Japanese)*

Cabinet Office, PKO hou seitei, sekou 20 shuunen (Twentieth Anniversary of establishment and enactment of PKO Act, Cabinet Office). https://www.cao.go.jp/pko/pko_j/info/other/other_data04.html
House of Councillors, Dai 196 Kokkai Sangiin Gaikou bouei iinkai dai 11 gou (Heisei 30 nen 4 gatsu 17 nichi) (Committee on Foreign Affairs and Defense, No. 11, April 17, 196 Diet, 2018). https://kokkai.ndl.go.jp/#/detail?minId=119613950X01120180417&spkNum=29&current%20%20=375
House of Representatives, Shitsumon honbun jouhou (Content of the question, Thursday, October 16, 2008). https://www.shugiin.go.jp/internet/itdb_shitsumon.nsf/html/shitsumon/a170131.htm
House of Representatives, Dai 193 Kokkai Shuugiin Yosan iinkai dai 12 gou (Heisei 29 nen 2 gatsu 17 nichi (Kin'you bi)) (Budget Committee, No. 12, Friday, February 17, 2017). https://www.shugiin.go.jp/internet/itdb_kaigiroku.nsf/html/kaigiroku/001819320170 217012.htm
Japan Pension Service, Nenkin kiroku mondai towa? (What is the pension record problem?). https://www.nenkin.go.jp/service/nenkinkiroku/torikumi/sonota/kini-cam/20150601-05.html
Japan Pension Service, Mitougou kiroku (5,095 man ken) no kaimei joukyou (Current situation of investigation on 50,950,000 unintegrated pension records). https://www.nenkin.go.jp/service/nenkinkiroku/torikumi/torikumijokyo/20150501.files/00000291543ecbUY2Wvn.pdf
Japan Pension Service, Kiroku no more ga ooku hakkennsareru pataan rei (Frequently found cases of record mis-integration). https://www.nenkin.go.jp/service/nenkinkiroku/torikumi/sonota/kini-cam/20150601-05.files/0000009880OnzusK6XWO.pdf
Ministry of Defense, Kokusai heiwa kyouryokuhou ni tsuite (About the International Peace Cooperation Act). https://www.mod.go.jp/j/approach/kokusai_heiwa/common/pdf/law_pko.pdf
Ministry of Finance, Kessai bunsho ni kansuru chousa ni tsuite (About the investigation of approval documents). https://www.mof.go.jp/public_relations/statement/other/search_kessaibunsho.htm
Ministry of Foreign Affairs, PKO seisaku Q and A (Q and A about PKO Policies). https://www.mofa.go.jp/mofaj/gaiko/pko/q_a.html
National Archives of Japan, Okinawa no henkan (Return of Okinawa). https://www.archives.go.jp/exhibition/digital/high-growth/contents/23/index.html
NHK Archives, Taiheiyou sensou to kuushuu (Pacific War and Air Raids, NHK Archives). https://www2.nhk.or.jp/archives/articles/?id=C0060015

# Chapter 2
# Progress and Problems of Records Management Laws in Japan: A Gap Between the Archival System and Information Laws

**Junta Okada**

**Abstract** This article explores the development and shortcomings of records management laws in Japan, focusing on the conceptual and institutional gap between archival systems and information law. Although the 2009 Public Records and Archives Management Act was a significant legislative step, Japanese legal scholarship has largely overlooked archives as a key component of democratic infrastructure. Most information law discourse prioritizes individual rights, neglecting the structural role of archives in transparency and accountability. By highlighting the democratic function of archives, this study argues for their fuller integration into information law frameworks and calls for interdisciplinary approaches to support transparency, public trust, and legal oversight.

**Keywords** Public records and archives management act (PRAM) · Information law · National archives of Japan · Administrative information act · Personal-rights-based theories · Democratic recordkeeping · Official-use properties · Public-use properties

## 2.1 Introduction

Over the past two decades, Japan's archival system and records management laws have undergone significant evolution. A landmark development was the enactment of the Public Records and Archives Management Act in 2009 (PRAM Act 2009).[1] These legal frameworks govern the acquisition, creation, use, preservation, and

[1] Public Records and Archives Management Act (English version); *available at* https://www.japaneselawtranslation.go.jp/en/laws/view/2790/en (last retrieved 1 May 2025).

J. Okada (✉)
Faculty of Law, Dokkyo University, Saitama, Japan
e-mail: junta@dokkyo.ac.jp



K. Fujiyoshi (ed.), *Governance, Ignorance, and Archives*,
https://doi.org/10.1007/978-981-95-1962-0_2

disposal of information by government bodies. As such, archival legislation should be regarded as a critical pillar within the broader spectrum of information law, alongside privacy law, freedom of information law, and national security regulations.

Despite this, most Japanese constitutional law textbooks—while emphasizing the foundational role of information law in a liberal democratic society—pay little attention to archival law. This reveals a substantial gap between the archival system and the broader information law framework.

This chapter explores the causes of this disconnect and proposes potential strategies to bridge the gap, aiming to enhance the democratic function of public records management.

## 2.2 Development of Records Management Laws in Japan

Following the Meiji Restoration in the late nineteenth century, the Japanese government underwent a comprehensive modernization process, which included the establishment of centralized administrative organs modeled after Western governmental structures. In this newly modernized bureaucracy, each ministry and agency was primarily responsible for managing its own administrative documents. These records included internal memos, policy drafts, correspondence, and other documentation generated in the course of governmental operations. However, there was no overarching or unified system for recordkeeping across the different governmental entities, and archival practices varied widely in quality and scope depending on the individual ministry.

Before this period, during the Edo Shogunate (1603–1867), the Tokugawa government had maintained its own style of recordkeeping,[2] but with the fall of the Shogunate and the formation of the modern nation-state, those records required preservation under the new regime. In 1885, when the Cabinet system was officially established, the Cabinet Library (Naikaku Bunko) was established to collect and maintain historical materials including ancient Japanese and Chinese books and collections. This institution became one of the earliest attempts by the modern Japanese government to institutionalize archival functions at the national level.

In the post–World War II era, the volume and complexity of administrative documentation increased dramatically. During this period, the traditional notion that "government records belong to the generating government department or agency" was transformed into the idea that "government records are the assets of the people," according to Mr. Iwakura, former Director of the National Archives of Japan[3].

This surge in public records introduced heightened risks: documents became scattered across agencies, were frequently misplaced, and, in some cases, were lost

[2] The Momijiyama Bunko was established in 1602 by Tokugawa Ieyasu, the founder of the Edo Shogunate. *See* https://db2.sido.keio.ac.jp/momijiyama/about_momijiyama (last retrieved 1 May 2025).

[3] Iwakura (1978), p. 76.

altogether. There was a growing awareness that, without proper systems for preservation and access, valuable administrative and historical records could be irretrievably lost.

Recognizing these risks, in November 1959, the Science Council of Japan—an advisory body composed of leading scholars and scientists—formally recommended to the Prime Minister that the government take concrete steps to establish a national archival institution.[4] This recommendation marked a critical moment in the recognition of records management and archival preservation as matters of public concern and scholarly importance.

In the wake of this recommendation, the government undertook studies on both domestic practices and international archival systems. Comparative research was conducted into how various countries—including the United States, United Kingdom, France, and Germany—organized their national archives, implemented public access policies, and established legal safeguards to prevent document destruction. Based on these studies and domestic evaluations, the National Archives of Japan was finally established in July 1971.[5]

However, the institutional framework under which the National Archives was created was legally modest. Rather than being established through a standalone National Archives Act, it was created through a revision of the Act for Establishment of the Prime Minister's Office (Act No. 127 of 1949).[6] As a result, the Archives was positioned as a relatively minor sub-organization within the Prime Minister's Office. Its administrative independence, legal authority, and budgetary capacity were limited. Although the creation of the National Archives was an important step forward, its capacity to lead a national records management policy or enforce best practices across ministries was inherently constrained from the beginning.

A more robust legal step occurred in 1987 with the enactment of the Public Archives Act (Act No. 115 of 1987). This Act explicitly acknowledged the value of public records and archives as part of the nation's historical heritage. Article 1 set out the Act's primary purpose: to preserve and provide access to public records and archives for public use and historical research. Article 3 extended the responsibility of managing important public records not only to the central government but also to local public entities. While this law helped to strengthen the normative foundation for preserving historical records, it remained oriented toward their cultural and historical significance rather than their functional or democratic value in governance and transparency.

In 1998, a new annex building was constructed to expand the physical storage capacity of the National Archives. This infrastructural development was followed in 1999 by the enactment of the National Archives Act (Act No. 79), which finally

---

[4] Science Council of Japan, *Preventing Dissipation of Public Records* (28 Nov. 1959) (in Japanese); *available at* https://www.scj.go.jp/ja/info/kohyo/02/04-62-k.pdf (last retrieved 1 May 2025).

[5] National Archives of Japan, *Outline of the National Archives* (web site); *available at* https://www.archives.go.jp/english/abouts/outline.html (last retrieved 1 May 2025).

[6] Act Partially Amending the Act for Establishment of the Prime Minister's Office (Act No.16 of 1971).

provided a specific legal basis for the institution. The Act stipulated the mission and responsibilities of the National Archives, further clarifying its role. Still, the legislative emphasis was placed squarely on the preservation of historical materials, with limited reference to archives as tools of democratic governance or public accountability.

Throughout this period, individual ministries and agencies continued to exercise primary responsibility for producing, managing, and transferring their own inactive or historical documents to the National Archives. This decentralized structure resulted in uneven practices and a lack of standardization. Moreover, the absence of an integrated oversight mechanism left open the possibility of selective preservation, delayed transfer, or even destruction of politically sensitive materials.

A significant turning point came with the enactment of the PRAM Act in 2009. For the first time, this law provided a comprehensive legal framework for managing public records across their entire life cycle—from creation and use to transfer, preservation, and public access. It also articulated, more clearly than previous laws, the relationship between recordkeeping and democratic governance. In this sense, the PRAM Act represented not only a policy innovation but also a symbolic shift in how Japan viewed the purpose and function of public records: no longer merely historical relics, but as integral to transparency, accountability, and citizens' trust in government.

## 2.3 Archives and Information Law in Japan: The Missing Pillar of Democratic Governance

The enactment of the PRAM Act in 2009 marked a significant milestone in Japan's efforts to institutionalize government accountability and transparency through legal frameworks governing records management. Importantly, this legislation did not emerge in isolation. It was developed in close alignment with the Act on Access to Information Held by Administrative Organs (Act No.42 of 1999), commonly referred to as the Administrative Information Act of 1999.[7] Together, these two laws constitute a dual foundation for open government in Japan—one concerned with ensuring citizens' access to information and the other with guaranteeing the systematic creation, preservation, and management of that information in the first place.

During the legislative process leading up to the PRAM Act's passage, government officials, policymakers, and experts repeatedly emphasized the intrinsic connection between archives and democracy. They argued that records are not merely operational tools for bureaucrats or historical artifacts for researchers but essential components of democratic governance. Proper records management, they asserted, ensures that governmental decisions can be traced, reviewed, and, if necessary,

[7] Act on Access to Information Held by Administrative Organs (English version); *available at* https://www.japaneselawtranslation.go.jp/en/laws/view/3765 (last retrieved 1 May 2025).

scrutinized or challenged. This framing placed the National Archives of Japan in a new light—not simply as a cultural or historical institution, but as a cornerstone of public accountability and constitutional government.

Despite these legislative intentions and the rhetorical support for archives as democratic infrastructure, the Japanese legal academic community has been slow to incorporate archival theory into the broader framework of information law. Most legal scholarship in Japan that addresses "information law" tends to center on freedom of information, data protection, and privacy—issues that are closely tied to individual rights and civil liberties. As a result, the equally critical function of archives has been largely overlooked in both theoretical analyses and practical discourse.

Information law itself is an interdisciplinary and still-maturing field, encompassing an increasingly diverse array of topics. In contemporary Japanese legal studies, it often includes issues such as protection of personal data, intellectual property rights, media regulation, internet governance, cybersecurity, and even legal implications of artificial intelligence. A common thread uniting these topics is their grounding in personal-rights-based theories, most of which are interpreted through the lens of the Japanese Constitution. For example, the right to know—understood as a derivative of the freedom of expression guaranteed by Article 21 of the Constitution—forms the basis of arguments for access to government-held information. Similarly, the right to privacy (Article 13) underpins data protection regimes, while Article 29 on property rights provides the constitutional justification for laws related to intellectual property.

However, such personal-rights-based approaches, while powerful in many contexts, are poorly equipped to account for the institutional and structural dimensions of democratic governance—particularly those pertaining to the management of public records.[8] Archives, by their very nature, operate at a collective and systemic level. They are not merely repositories of private information or proprietary data, but organized systems that enable society to monitor, evaluate, and understand the workings of its government over time. In this regard, archival systems serve a public, rather than individual, function. Their significance lies in their ability to preserve institutional memory, provide evidence of government activity, and support transparency and legal accountability.

The failure to fully integrate archival studies into the conceptual framework of information law creates a serious blind spot. It results in an incomplete understanding of what is required to ensure government openness and integrity. Without a robust legal and theoretical foundation that recognizes the central role of archives, public records risk being treated as secondary or ancillary to other information concerns. This not only marginalizes the archival function but also weakens the broader project of democratic governance.

In short, while the PRAM Act of 2009 represents an important step toward recognizing the role of archives in a democratic society, the academic and legal

[8] Okada (2021a), pp. 18–19.

discourse surrounding information law in Japan is yet to catch up. To move forward, it is necessary to rethink the boundaries of information law to include not only rights-based perspectives but also institutional and procedural dimensions that acknowledge the foundational role of archives in sustaining democratic accountability.

## 2.4 Identifying the Structural Problem: Archival Silence in Japanese Legal Discourse

Despite the democratic aspirations embedded in the PRAM Act of 2009, a major structural issue persists in the academic and institutional landscape of Japan's information governance: the systematic neglect of archives and records management within legal scholarship, particularly in the field of information law. This omission is not merely a matter of academic oversight—it reveals a deeper conceptual disconnect between the theoretical development of information law and the practical needs of democratic recordkeeping.

A cursory survey of recent Japanese legal textbooks reveals this imbalance clearly. Numerous publications use the term "Information Law" in their titles, indicating a growing academic interest in this interdisciplinary field. However, a closer look at their contents shows a striking absence of dedicated chapters or even substantial sections addressing archives or public records management [Table 2.1]. One might expect that such texts would treat archives as foundational to transparency and accountability—core values in any democratic information system—but this is rarely the case.

Even notable contributions, such as those by Professor Uzaki, whose collected writings engage deeply with topics in information governance, fail to give archives their due weight. Moreover, popular legal education resources like Hōgaku Kyōshitsu—a respected monthly magazine on legal studies—featured a special issue on information law in August 2020.[9] While this issue covered a broad spectrum of topics, including privacy, AI, and media regulation, it conspicuously excluded any discussion of archives or the legal frameworks surrounding public records. This silence reflects a broader trend in Japanese information law: the theory and institutional framework surrounding archives remain insufficiently recognized and under-theorized.

The consequences of this neglect are not merely academic. They impact how laws are interpreted, enforced, and improved in practice. A telling example of this theoretical gap can be found in the writings of Supreme Court Justice Katsuya Uga, a former professor of administrative law at the University of Tokyo. Justice Uga has acknowledged the legal shift brought about by the PRAM Act, noting that public

[9] The special issue of Hōgaku Kyōshitsu titled "*The Frontier of Information Law*" features nine articles spanning approximately 40 pages.

**Table 2.1** Recent Japanese Textbooks using the words "Information Law (情報法)" in the Title

| | Title of Chapter refers to Archives or Public Record | Pages | Lines |
|---|---|---|---|
| Uga and Hasebe (2012) | Disclosure of Administrative Information | pp. 86–87 | 27 |
| Hayashi (2017) | Information as Subject to Legal Regulation | pp. 105–106 | 30 |
| Sogabe et al. (2019) | Personal Data Protection | p. 241 | 10 |
| Mizutani (2022) | Disclosure of Administrative Information | pp. 55–56 | 53 |
| Komukai (2022) | Treatment of Information and Legal Responsibility | pp. 165–166 | 31 |
| Tomooka (2022) | Disclosure of Administrative Information and Personal Data Protection | pp. 223–233 | 65 |
| Yoneyama (2022) | Disclosure of Administrative Information | p. 87 | 15 |
| Kodama (2023) | Disclosure of Administrative Information and Personal Data Protection | pp. 150–151 | 14 |
| Uzaki (2024) | Legal System of the Public Records Management | pp. 2–54 | 1664 |

records have transitioned from being classified as kōyōbutsu (official-use properties) to kōkyōyōbutsu (public-use properties)[10]. Official-use properties refer to assets used exclusively for governmental activities, such as government office buildings and police vehicles. Public-use properties, on the other hand, refer to assets made available for public use, such as parks, roads, and bridges. This distinction—rooted in administrative law theory influenced by German legal scholarship—implies that public records are no longer merely tools for internal governmental use, but resources that should be accessible to society at large.

While this reconceptualization is accurate and significant, Justice Uga's approach still reflects a narrow view of archives. His analysis focuses on their legal classification and access rights, but does not explore the deeper civic function of archives in supporting participatory democracy, ensuring intergenerational accountability, and enabling investigative journalism or historical inquiry. The archive is reduced to a passive "storage" facility, rather than understood as an active institution of governance.

This limited conception stands in contrast to the more ambitious vision outlined by the 2008 Advisory Council on Public Records Management. In its official report, the Council proposed a holistic framework for managing public records throughout their entire life cycle—from creation and use to long-term preservation and public access. The report called for a governance system that would monitor records management practices across all government ministries, ideally under the supervision of an external, independent agency.[11] The National Archives of Japan was identified as

---

[10] Katsuya Uga, Jōhō kōkai to kōbunsho kanri [INFORMATION DISCLOSURE AND PUBLIC RECORDS MANAGEMENT] (Yuhikaku, 2010) p.2. [in Japanese].

[11] Advisory Council on Public Records Management, *Final Report* (4 Nov. 2008) (in Japanese); *available at* https://www.cas.go.jp/jp/seisaku/koubun/hokoku.pdf (last retrieved 1 May 2025).

a potentially suitable institution for this oversight role, provided it could be restructured and empowered accordingly.

Unfortunately, the political developments of the 2010s revealed the fragility of this vision. During the administration of Prime Minister Shinzō Abe, several high-profile incidents came to light involving the concealment, falsification, or unlawful destruction of public records.[12] These scandals highlighted the weaknesses in the existing legal and institutional safeguards. Under the current framework, if the Prime Minister or other high-ranking officials choose to ignore or condone such misconduct, there are few effective means to correct it from outside the government. The current design of the PRAM Act does not equip the National Archives—or any other body—with the authority or independence needed to investigate or sanction violations robustly.

The broader implication is that without a system of independent oversight and comprehensive archival governance, records management becomes vulnerable to politicization and manipulation. Democratic accountability depends not only on citizens' formal rights to request information but also on the structural assurance that public records are being preserved, maintained, and disclosed with integrity. In the absence of such guarantees, even the strongest freedom of information laws risk becoming hollow.

Thus, the root problem is not simply a lack of laws or institutions, but a conceptual failure to understand archives as integral to democratic infrastructure. This failure has practical consequences—ranging from the erosion of public trust to the weakening of institutional memory—and will persist until the legal academy, policymakers, and the broader public recognize the civic function of archives in the same way they do other pillars of democratic governance.

## 2.5 Conclusion: Toward a Normative Framework for Archival Governance in a Democratic Society

The enactment of the Public Records and Archives Management Act (PRAM Act) in 2009 was a landmark achievement in the development of Japan's information governance system. It symbolized a shift from viewing public records merely as administrative instruments to recognizing them as civic assets—essential to ensuring transparency, accountability, and institutional memory in a democratic society. However, over a decade later, significant challenges remain in both the implementation and theoretical integration of this legislative framework.

Under the current legal and administrative structure, the National Archives of Japan holds responsibility primarily for receiving and preserving inactive or historically valuable public records—those no longer in active use by government

[12] *Part of "Moritomo Documents" Disclosed to Widow of MOF Official*, Jiji (4 Apr. 2025); *available at* https://sp.m.jiji.com/english/show/39293 (last retrieved 1 May 2025).

ministries and agencies.[13] Its role is largely limited to the post-use phase of document life cycles. It lacks the authority to intervene in how records are created, classified, managed, or disposed of while still within the administrative sphere. As a result, the Archives operates downstream in a system where upstream mismanagement—such as the improper deletion, falsification, or concealment of documents—can go unchecked.

What is urgently needed is a normative and institutional framework that embeds archival logic throughout the entire record-keeping process. Archives should not be understood simply as physical repositories or bureaucratic endpoints, but as normative institutions with a mandate to support democratic governance.[14] This involves granting them legal authority and institutional independence to oversee records management practices across the public sector. It also requires the creation of mechanisms for accountability, including the power to audit record-keeping, enforce compliance, and investigate misconduct.

Furthermore, the development of robust archival governance must be matched by a corresponding evolution in academic theory. Merely enacting laws is not sufficient; legal theory must evolve to provide the conceptual foundations for those laws to be meaningfully interpreted, defended, and improved. In Japan, the academic field of information law is still in a formative stage. While it has rapidly expanded to encompass cutting-edge issues such as artificial intelligence, data privacy, and media regulation, it is yet to engage deeply with archives as a subject of legal and democratic significance.

This lacuna reflects a broader epistemological issue. Much of Japanese information law scholarship has been framed through the lens of personal rights—focusing on individual privacy, access to information, and intellectual property. While these dimensions are undoubtedly important, they are insufficient for understanding archives, which function less as instruments of personal empowerment and more as structural enablers of collective accountability. Archives are not about the "right to know" in the abstract, but about ensuring that institutions can be held responsible, that truth can be verified, and that historical records are available to future generations.

Bridging this gap will require interdisciplinary collaboration between legal scholars, archivists, historians, and practitioners of public administration. Expertise in archival science must be integrated into the formulation and interpretation of legal norms. Likewise, legal scholars must begin to appreciate the constitutional dimensions of record-keeping and the pivotal role archives play in preserving democratic legitimacy.

Finally, the future of archival governance in Japan hinges not only on legislative reform but also on cultural transformation. Legal scholars, lawmakers, and civil society must come to see archives not as peripheral technical institutions, but as

[13] Okada (2021b), pp. 41–42.

[14] National Archives, U.K., *Our Research Vision 2024-27*, p.3; *available at* https://cdn.nationalarchives.gov.uk/documents/the-national-archives-research-vision-2024-27.pdf (last retrieved 1 May 2025).

central pillars of democratic society. Only through such a reorientation can Japan build a system in which government records are preserved not just for bureaucratic continuity, but for public trust, historical integrity, and civic empowerment.

## References

Hayashi K (2017) Jōhō-hō no legal mind [The Legal Mind of Information Law]. Keiso Shobo [in Japanese]

Iwakura N (1978) Archives of Japan. Archivaria Nov.7 Winter, p 76

Kodama H (2023) Jōhō to hō [Information and Law]. Foundation for the Promotion of The Open University of Japan, [in Japanese]

Komukai T (2022) Jōhō-hō nyūmon: Digital network no hōritsu (Dai 6 han) [Introduction to Information Law: Legal Issues in the Digital Network Society (6th edn)] NTT Publishing. [in Japanese]

Mizutani E (2022) Readings media-hō / jōhō-hō [Readings in Media Law and Information Law]. Horitsu Bunka Sha [in Japanese]

Okada J (2021a) Archives in parliament: democratic role of the Japanese national diet library. In: Fujiyoshi K (ed) Archives for maintaining community and society in digital age. Springer, pp 18–19

Okada J (2021b) Meanings of archivist in the Japanese Constitution. In: Fujiyoshi K (ed) Archives, accountability, and democracy in the digital age. Springer, pp 41–42

Sogabe M et al. (2019) Jōhō-hō gaisetsu (Dai 2 han) [Introduction to Information Law (2nd edn.)] Kobundo [in Japanese]

Tomooka F (2022) Gyōsei jōhō hōsei no gendaiteki kōzō [The Contemporary Structure of Administrative Information Law]. Shinzansha [in Japanese]

Uga K, Hasebe Y (2012) Jōhō-hō [Information Law]. Yuhikaku [in Japanese]

Uzaki M (2024) Jōhō hōsei no ronten: Kōbunsho kanri, jōhō kōkai, kojin jōhō hogo [Key Issues in Information Law: Public Records Management, Freedom of Information, and Personal Data Protection]. Nihon Hyoron Sha, [in Japanese]

Yoneyama T (2022) 18-sai kara hajimeru jōhō-hō (Dai 2 han) [Information Law for 18-Year-Olds (2nd edn)]. Horitsu Bunka Sha. [in Japanese]

# Chapter 3
# Archives in National Constitutions

**Satoshi Yokodaido**

**Abstract** While archives are widely recognized as essential for democratic governance, namely, ensuring transparency, accountability, and collective memory, they are rarely treated as constitutional objects. However, around 30 of the world's nearly 200 constitutions mention archives explicitly. This chapter examines the underexplored role of archives in national constitutions and attempts to categorize these references into four functional categories: Rights, Authority and Duty, Value, and Existence. This chapter concludes by linking archives to broader themes of mnemonic constitutionalism and institutional integrity.

**Keywords** Right to access personal information · Individual identity · Dignity · And rights · Continuity and jurisdictional clarity · Nation's collective memory and identity · Cultural heritage · National identity · Transparency · Ethical governance

## 3.1 Introduction

The Universal Declaration of Archives in 2011 states, "Archives record decisions, actions and memories. Archives are a unique and irreplaceable heritage passed from one generation to another. Archives are managed from creation to preserve their value and meaning. They are authoritative sources of information underpinning accountable and transparent administrative actions. They play an essential role in the development of societies by safeguarding and contributing to individual and community memory. Open access to archives enriches our knowledge of human society, promotes democracy, protects citizens' rights and enhances the quality of life.[1]

[1] https://www.ica.org/resource/universal-declaration-on-archives-uda/.

S. Yokodaido (✉)
Law School, Keio University, Tokyo, Japan
e-mail: yokodai@keio.jp



K. Fujiyoshi (ed.), *Governance, Ignorance, and Archives*,
https://doi.org/10.1007/978-981-95-1962-0_3

Despite their recognized importance in a democratic society, archives have rarely been examined from a constitutional perspective in Japan.[2] The Japanese Constitution of 1946 contains virtually no explicit reference to archives or the practice of record-keeping, except as a Legislative record.[3] This constitutional silence may help explain the lack of interest in archives as a constitutional issue in Japan.

This raises the broader question: How do other national constitutions address the issue of archives? Approximately 200 constitutions are currently in force worldwide. According to data from the *Constitute Project*,[4] a comprehensive database offering English translations of national constitutions, roughly 30 of these constitutions explicitly mention the term "archives.[5]" In order to analyze how archives are addressed in national constitutions, this chapter undertakes a typological classification of relevant provisions. The aim is not to propose a normative model or to evaluate the adequacy of existing constitutional language, but rather to organize and present a comparative overview of the ways in which constitutions refer to archives. To this end, I classify the references into four functional categories: (1) *Rights*, where individuals are granted access to or control over information held in archives; (2) *Authority and Duty*, where constitutional texts allocate legislative or administrative responsibilities for archival management; (3) *Value*, where archives are recognized as elements of national cultural or historical heritage; and (4) *Existence*, where constitutions merely acknowledge the presence of archives without attaching specific rights, duty, or obligations. These categories are provisional in nature, and individual constitutional provisions may span multiple functions or overlap between categories. By presenting this classification, the chapter aims to provide a conceptual map of constitutional references to archives. This, in turn, serves as a foundation for future inquiry into the democratic, administrative, and cultural significance of archives within constitutional orders.

## 3.2 Archives and Individual Rights

Several national constitutions explicitly mention archives in connection with protecting individual rights. These provisions typically recognize the right of individuals to access, review, and request the correction of personal data held in archival or

---

[2] Okada (2021). Yokodaido (2023), p. 15.

[3] Article 57, paragraph 2 of the Constitution of Japan explicitly provides that "Each House shall keep a record of proceedings. This record shall be published and given general circulation, excepting such parts of proceedings of secret session as may be deemed to require secrecy." The term "archives" used in this chapter primarily refers to administrative records.

[4] https://www.constituteproject.org/.

[5] Since different constitutions may use varying terminology, and because this survey does not aim to offer a comprehensive analysis, the number of cases presented here should be regarded as provisional.

official repositories. Such rights are often embedded within broader data protection frameworks, transparency, and administrative accountability.

For instance, Article 69(1) of the 2010 Constitution of Angola guarantees the right to file a writ of habeas data, ensuring that individuals can access information about themselves stored in archives and computerized records, as well as the right to demand its correction or update, subject to legal exceptions such as state or legal secrecy.[6] Article 200(4) of the same constitution reinforces this by guaranteeing access to archives and administrative records more generally, again subject to similar legal exceptions.[7] The Constitution of Cape Verde (1980, rev. 1992)[8] and Guatemala (1985, rev. 1993)[9] similarly establish a constitutional right to access personal information, recognizing knowledge of its content and intended use, as well as the right to request corrections. Cuba's 2019 Constitution, in Article 97, provides for an individual's right to access, correct, or request deletion of personal data in archives or public databases.[10] Similarly, the 1992 Estonian Constitution (rev. 2015) affirms both the right to public information and access to personal data held by state institutions, including archives, though this right may be lawfully restricted under specific circumstances such as the protection of others' rights or criminal investigation.[11] Mozambique's Constitution can also be placed within the "Rights" category,

[6] Const. of Angola, arts. 69(1) (2010): "Everyone shall have to right to apply for a writ of habeas data to ensure that they are informed of any information about them contained in files, archives and computerised records, and that they are informed of the purpose for which this is destined and, in addition, shall have the right to demand that these are corrected or updated, under the terms of the law and whilst safeguarding state and legal secrecy.

[7] Const. of Angola, arts. 200(4) (2010): "Individuals shall be guaranteed the right to access archives and administrative records, without prejudice to the legal provisions for security and defence matters, state secrecy, criminal investigation and personal privacy."

[8] Const. of Cape Verde, art. 43(1) (1980, as amended 1992): "All citizens shall have the right to access to information, to be aware of computer files, archives, and records which relate to them, as well as the right to be informed of their purpose and use in order to request the correction or updating of the data."

[9] Const. of Guatemala, art. 31 (1985, as amended 1993): "All persons have the right to take cognizance of what the archives, records, or any other form of State registries contain about them, and [regarding] the purpose for which such data is used, as well as their correction, rectification, and updating [actualización]. Registries and records of political affiliation, except for those pertaining to the electoral authorities and to the political parties[,] are prohibited."

[10] Const. of Cuba, art. 97 (2019): "The State recognizes the right of all people to access their personal information in public registries, archives, or other databases, as well as request its non-disclosure or obtain a due correction, rectification, modification, update, or deletion.

[11] Const. of Estonia, art. 44, paras. 1–3 (1992, as amended 2015): "Constitution of Estonia, art. 44, paras. 1–3 (1992, rev. 2015): Everyone has the right to freely obtain information disseminated for public use." Para 2 "All state agencies, local governments, and their officials have a duty to provide information about their activities, pursuant to procedure provided by law, to an Estonian citizen at his or her request, except information the disclosure of which is prohibited by law, and information intended exclusively for internal use." Para 3 "An Estonian citizen has the right to access information about himself or herself held in state agencies and local governments and in state and local government archives, pursuant to procedure provided by law. This right may be restricted pursuant to law to protect the rights and freedoms of others or the confidentiality of a child's filiation, and

but in a restrictive, privacy-oriented sense. Article 71(3) of the Mozambique Constitution prohibits unauthorized access to third-party personal data held in archives or databases, focusing on privacy protection rather than guaranteeing a general right of access. Thus, it reflects a more defensive form of rights protection compared to constitutions that affirmatively guarantee information access.[12] Paragraph 1 of Article 68 of the Egyptian Constitution is also categorized as the "Rights" category, as it affirms that official information, data, and records are the property of the people and guarantees a constitutional right of access and transparency.[13] It establishes a legal entitlement for citizens to obtain such information and mandates the state to facilitate access and provide remedies against unjustified denials.

These constitutional provisions reflect a shared normative commitment: archives are not merely state instruments for institutional memory or historical recordkeeping, but are also repositories of individual identity, dignity, and rights. By embedding rights of access and correction into constitutional texts, these countries acknowledge archives as legal sites where the individual and the state intersect. However, the issue arises when such constitutions focus solely on individual rights and fail to fully recognize the public role of archives and their overall contribution to democracy. If archives function merely as a tool for protecting personal information, their fundamental significance—the role of promoting government transparency and accountability—risks being overlooked.

---

in the interests of combating a criminal offence, apprehending a criminal offender, or ascertaining the truth in a criminal procedure.

[12] Const. of Mozambique, art. 71(3) (2004, as amended 2007): "Access to data bases or to computerised archives, files and records for obtaining information on the personal data of third parties, as well as the transfer of personal data from one computerised file to another that belongs to a distinct service or institution, shall be prohibited except in cases provided for by law or by judicial decision."

[13] Const. of Egypt, art. 68, para. 1 (2014, as amended 2019): Para 1, "Information, data, statistics and official documents are owned by the people. Disclosure thereof from various sources is a right guaranteed by the state to all citizens. The state shall provide and make them available to citizens with transparency. The law shall organize rules for obtaining such, rules of availability and confidentiality, rules for depositing and preserving such, and lodging complaints against refusals to grant access thereto. The law shall specify penalties for withholding information or deliberately providing false information."

## 3.3 Archives as a Matter of State Power and Institutional Duty

Beyond individual rights, a significant number of constitutions also address archives in terms of state authority and institutional obligations. In these provisions, archives are not merely passive repositories of memory, but are positioned as objects of governance—matters to be regulated, funded, and administered by public institutions in accordance with constitutional principles. It can be said that these articles reflect a conception of archives as vital infrastructure for democratic oversight, cultural preservation, and bureaucratic continuity.

In particular, many federal constitutions include specific provisions clarifying the allocation of responsibility between federal and subnational units. For example, Nigeria's 1999 Constitution (rev. 2011) provides a clear legislative framework in which both the National Assembly and State Houses of Assembly are empowered to legislate with respect to archives and public records. At the same time, it contains a safeguard clause ensuring the preservation of all archival materials existing at the time of the Constitution's commencement, thereby emphasizing continuity and jurisdictional clarity.[14] Similarly, the Mexican Constitution (1917, rev. 2015) authorizes the federal Congress to enact a general law creating a coordinated and harmonized system for organizing and managing archival records across all levels of government, including federal, local, and municipal authorities.[15] This framework ensures institutional coherence while maintaining the national character of archival governance. Other federal or quasi-federal states adopt comparable mechanisms. In South Africa (1996, rev. 2012), Schedule 5 assigns exclusive competence over non-national archives to the provincial level.[16] South Sudan's Constitution (2011, rev. 2013) also includes "state archives" within the list of powers devolved to the states.[17] Spain's Constitution (1978, rev. 2011) assigns the State exclusive competence over the protection of its cultural and artistic heritage, including archives belonging to

---

[14] Const. of Nigeria, pt. II, Concurrent Legislative List, paras. 4–6 (1999, as amended 2011): "4. The National Assembly may make laws for the Federation or any part thereof with respect to the archives and public records of the Federation." "5. A House of Assembly may, subject to paragraph 4 hereof, make laws for that State or any part thereof with respect to archives and public records of the Government of the State." "6. Nothing in paragraphs 4 and 5 hereof shall be construed as enabling any laws to be made which do not preserve the archives and records which are in existence at the date of commencement of this Constitution, and which are kept by authorities empowered to do so in any part of the Federation."

[15] Const. of Mexico, art. 73, cl. XXIX-T (1917, as amended 2015): " To issue a general law that establishes a homogenous and coordinated system to organize and manage all the files and documents at the federal, local and municipal level including the Federal District and its political subdivisions. This law must describe the organization and functions of the National Archives System."

[16] Const. of South Africa, sch. 5, pt. A (1996, rev. 2012): (Functional Areas of Exclusive Provincial Legislative Competence) "Archives other than national archives."

[17] Const. of South Sudan, sch. B, 34: "The exclusive executive and legislative powers of a state shall be as follows: [...] 34 State archives, antiquities and monuments."

the State, although their management may be delegated to the Autonomous Communities.[18]

Beyond federal contexts, some constitutions assign archival responsibilities to specific national institutions. In Lesotho, Article 104(2) mandates the College of Chiefs to safeguard the national archives within the scope of its constitutional functions.[19] Uganda's Constitution (1995, rev. 2017) similarly lists "archives and public records" among the functions of central government.[20] Article 10(1)(13) of Austria's Constitution includes archival services among the matters reserved for the Federation, particularly those related to science and the arts, indicating a subject-matter-specific allocation of authority.[21] Finally, Zambia's Constitution (1991, rev. 2016) categorizes national archives as an exclusive national function within its system of devolved governance, reaffirming the central role of archival policy in national administration.[22] The Constitution of Egypt (2014, rev. 2019) addresses archives in both rights-based and institutional terms. While Paragraph 1 of Article 68 is classified under the "Rights" category for establishing access and transparency as constitutional entitlements,[23] Paragraph 2 falls within this category, as it imposes affirmative obligations on state institutions to transfer official documents to the National Library and Archives, ensure their protection against loss or damage, and undertake restoration and digitization using modern technologies.[24] These provisions establish a constitutional duty of care in managing and preserving archival materials.

Through these examples, it becomes clear that archives are not only seen as valuable cultural or informational assets but also as constitutional objects of public authority. In both centralized and federal systems, constitutions define the actors

---

[18] Const. of Spain, art. 149(1)(28a) (1978, as amended 2011): "The State shall have exclusive competence over the following matters: [...] 28a Protection of Spain's cultural and artistic heritage and national monuments against exportation and spoliation; museums, libraries, and archives belonging to the State, without prejudice to their management by the Self-governing Communities."

[19] Const. of Lesotho, art. 104(2) (1993, as amended 2018): "The College of Chiefs shall have the functions conferred on it by section 45 and section 46 of this Constitution and the duty to maintain and safeguard the national archives in relation to those functions, and it shall also have such other functions as may be conferred on it by any other law."

[20] Const. of Uganda, sixth sched., Art. 189 (1995, as amended 2017). Functions and Sercices for which Government is Responsible (Article 189): National monuments, antiquities, archives and public records, as Parliament may determine.

[21] Const. of Austria, art. 10(1)(13) (1920): "The Federation has powers of legislation and execution in the following matters: [...]13 archive and library services for the sciences and specialist purposes; matters pertaining to Federal collections and establishments serving the arts and sciences."

[22] Const. of Zambia, Anenex, (1991, as amended 2016) ANNEX.:Functions of National Provincial and Local Levels of Devolved Government (Article 147(2)), A. Exclusive national functions, National archives."

[23] *See supra* note 13.

[24] Const. of Egypt, art. 68, para. 2 (2014, as amended 2019).: Para 2, "State institutions shall deposit official documents with the National Library and Archives once they are no longer in use. They shall also protect them, secure them from loss or damage, and restore and digitize them using all modern means and instruments, as per the law."

and levels of government responsible for managing, preserving, and regulating archives. This ensures legal clarity, promotes institutional accountability, and underscores the foundational role of archives in supporting transparent and stable governance.

## 3.4 The Value of Archives as Cultural and Historical Heritage

The third category of constitutional references to archives emphasizes their cultural and historical significance. This category may overlap with others, as cultural and historical value is often interwoven with legal governance and institutional responsibilities. In this context, archives are not primarily viewed as administrative instruments or subjects of legal governance, but as foundational components of a nation's collective memory and identity. Their preservation is tied to broader constitutional duties relating to cultural heritage, historical consciousness, and social cohesion.

This symbolic and cultural role of archives is clearly articulated in the 2008 Constitution of Ecuador (rev. 2021). Article 379(3) includes "documents, objects, collections, archives, libraries, and museums" among the tangible and intangible elements of cultural heritage that are "relevant for the memory and identity of persons and groups.[25]" This provision locates archives firmly within the scope of the state's obligation to protect cultural heritage, recognizing their enduring contribution to the continuity, reflection, and self-understanding of the national community. Spain's constitutional provision, which was mentioned above, also identifies archives as part of the nation's cultural heritage.[26]

A similar approach is found in the Constitution of Peru (1993, rev. 2021), which in Article 21 defines archival materials—alongside archaeological sites, monuments, and artistic works—as elements of the "cultural heritage of the Nation.".[27] This designation applies regardless of whether the materials are publicly or privately held, thereby underlining their public character and the corresponding obligation of the state to protect them. The constitutional protection afforded to archives here reflects not only their historical value but also their role in shaping and preserving national identity. Hungary's Constitution (2011, art. U(10)) offers a historically focused provision. It declares that documents created by the former com-

[25] Const. of Ecuador, art. 379(3) (2008, as amended 2021): "The following are part of the tangible and intangible cultural heritage that is relevant for the memory and identity of persons and groups and the target of safeguarding by the State, among others: 3 Documents, objects, collections, archives, libraries, and museums that have historical, artistic, archeological, ethnographic or paleontological value."

[26] *See supra* note 18.

[27] Const. of Peru, art. 21 (1993, as amended 2021): "Archeological sites and remains, constructions, monuments, places, bibliographical documents and archival materials, art objects, and tokens of historical value, expressly declared cultural assets and those provisionally presumed to be so, are the cultural heritage of the Nation, irrespective of whether they are private or public property. They are protected by the State."

munist regime and its affiliated organizations must be considered state property and deposited in public archives.[28] This reflects a transitional justice approach, where archival practice is constitutionally tied to democratic consolidation and historical reckoning.

These provisions recognize that Archives are no longer seen merely as tools for recording state actions or managing administrative processes. Instead, they are valued for their capacity to preserve the narratives, struggles, and achievements that constitute a nation's historical experience. They serve as constitutional sites of memory, enabling societies to critically engage with the past and foster a sense of shared identity and purpose. By enshrining the value of archives in their constitutions, states acknowledge that memory itself is a constitutional concern—an object of legal protection as well as cultural pride.[29]

## 3.5 Constitutional Recognition of the Existence of Archives

The fourth and final category consists of those constitutional provisions that, while not defining rights or assigning duties, nonetheless affirm the existence of archives through *indirect* references. Though indirect, such references could contribute to the constitutional visibility of archival institutions and underscore their role as custodians of key constitutional documents and state records. The constitutional relevance of such provisions may lie in the visibility they afford to archival institutions, indirectly affirming the state's recognition of archives as instruments that support political and legal continuity, even in the absence of explicit rights or institutional mandates.

In several countries, the preservation of foundational constitutional acts is expressly entrusted to national archival bodies. For example, the 1953 Constitution of Denmark (Part II, Article 8) requires that the King's declaration to uphold the Constitution be executed in two identical originals—one preserved by the Folketing and the other deposited in the Public Record Office.[30] While the provision does not

[28] Const. of Hungary, art. U(10) (2011, as amended 2016): "The documents of the communist state party, of the civil society organisations and youth organisations established with the contribution of or influenced directly by the communist state party, and of trade unions, created during the communist dictatorship shall be property of the State and shall be deposited in public archives in the same way as the files of organs performing public duties."

[29] Although the constitutions of countries such as Italy, South Korea, and Brazil do not explicitly use the term "archives," they may be understood to include public records and documents within the broader concept of cultural heritage. For instance, the Italian Constitution (Art. 9) refers to the protection of historical and artistic heritage, which has been interpreted through subsequent legislation to extend to archival materials. Similarly, South Korea's Constitution (Art. 9) and Brazil's Constitution (Art. 216) may be seen as associating public documents and historical records with the nation's cultural patrimony, thus potentially placing them under constitutional protection despite the absence of direct archival terminology.

[30] Const. of Denmark, pt. II, § 8 (1953): "The King, prior to his accession to the Throne, shall make a solemn Declaration in writing before the Council of State that he will faithfully adhere to the

elaborate on the nature or governance of the archive, it affirms its existence and legal function as a trusted repository of sovereign declarations. A similar provision appears in Iceland's Constitution (1944, rev. 2013, Article 10), which mandates that the President's oath of office be prepared in duplicate, with one copy deposited in the National Archives.[31] This simple procedural requirement attests to the institutional authority and symbolic centrality of archives in upholding constitutional continuity. Myanmar's 2008 Constitution (rev. 2015, Article 454) explicitly states that the authoritative Burmese-language text of the Constitution shall be preserved in the National Archives.[32] The provision adds that this archived version shall serve as conclusive evidence of the Constitution's contents—thereby assigning to the archival copy a definitive legal status. Here, the archive serves as both guardian and validator of the constitutional order. The Constitution of Paraguay (1992, rev. 2011) similarly provides for the preservation of records from the National Constituent Convention, including plenary session diaries and editorial commission minutes. Article 17 entrusts these materials to the Central Bank of the State on behalf of the Legislative Power, pending their official transfer to the National Archives.[33] Although framed as a transitional arrangement, the provision affirms the eventual and proper location of these foundational documents: the national archival institution.

These references also have some constitutional significance. They acknowledge the institutional role of archives within the framework of constitutional administration. Rather than serving solely as administrative repositories, archives in these contexts preserve key constitutional instruments such as foundational laws, oaths of office, and legislative records. By incorporating preservation duties into constitutional text, these provisions help ensure that constitutional continuity is supported through normative principles and institutionalized practices of record-keeping.

---

Constitution Act. Two identical originals of the Declaration shall be executed, one of which shall be handed over to the Folketing to be preserved in its archives, and the other shall be filed in the Public Record Office. Where the King, owing to his absence or for other reasons, is unable to sign the aforesaid Declaration immediately on his accession to the Throne, the government shall, unless otherwise provided by Statute, be conducted by the Council of State until such Declaration has been signed. Where the King already as Successor to the Throne has signed the aforesaid Declaration, he shall accede to the Throne immediately on its vacancy."

[31] Const. of Iceland, art. 10 (1944, as amended 2013): "On assuming office, the President shall take an oath or pledge to uphold the Constitution. Two identical originals shall be executed of this oath or pledge. One shall be kept by Althingi and the other by the National Archives."

[32] Constitution of Myanmar, art. 454 (2008, as amended 2015): "The Myanmar text of this Constitution shall be kept as record in the National Archives. Such text shall be conclusive evidence of the provisions of this Constitution."

[33] Const. of Paraguay, art. 17 (1992, as amended 2011): "The deposit and the conservation of all the documentation produced by the National Constituent Convention, such as diaries and acts and of plenary sessions and those of the Comisión Redactora [Editing Commission] will be entrusted to the Central Bank of the State, in the name of and at the disposal of the Legislative Power, until, by law, their remission to and storage at the National Archives is provided."

## 3.6 Analysis and Comment

Among approximately 200 constitutions currently in force worldwide, only about thirty (15%) make direct mention of the term "archives." These references vary considerably in form, content, and legal significance. In some cases, archives are mentioned in the context of access rights or institutional responsibilities. In others, they are treated as components of a nation's cultural heritage or as repositories of foundational legal and constitutional documents.

Given this variation, it would be premature to suggest the emergence of a general trend toward the constitutionalization of archives. The vast majority of constitutions remain silent on the issue, including the Constitution of Japan. Nevertheless, the presence of archival provisions in a subset of constitutions is not without significance. These references, modest though they may be, reflect a limited but discernible degree of legal and institutional recognition of archival functions. At the very least, they help identify which aspects of archival practice—such as preservation, authenticity, and institutional continuity—have attracted constitutional attention. They also offer valuable comparative material for scholars examining the intersection between constitutional design and information governance. In this light, constitutional references to archives may be seen not so much as declarations of strong normative commitments, but rather as acknowledgments of basic infrastructural assumptions underlying constitutional governance. Instead of presenting archives as rights-generating institutions, most provisions treat them as custodial or symbolic elements of the constitutional order.

The constitutional relevance of archives may also be viewed through the lens of mnemonic constitutionalism.[34] This emerging theoretical approach highlights the role of constitutions in shaping collective memory and preserving foundational narratives of political identity. Archives function as institutional spaces where the documentary traces of constitutional formation, conflict, and transformation are preserved and curated. In this sense, archives serve not merely to guarantee legal or administrative continuity but also to sustain the symbolic authority and historical legitimacy of constitutional orders. From this perspective, the inclusion of archival provisions in constitutions may be interpreted as an effort to institutionalize not only legal rules but also the memory of constitutional becoming—that is, the process by which constitutional meaning emerges over time through both events and recollection.

In addition, archives may be understood as a structural foundation for independent regulatory institutions, such as ombuds offices and anti-corruption commissions. These bodies require access to accurate and comprehensive records in order to fulfill their oversight mandates effectively. Some constitutional scholars have proposed the idea of a fourth "integrity branch" of government—alongside the

[34] *See e.g.,* Uladzislau Belavusau, *Final Thoughts on Mnemonic Constitutionalism* in VERFASSUNGSBLOG, January 15, 2018 (emphasis added). https://verfassungsblog.de/final-thoughts-on-mnemonic-constitutionalism/

legislative, executive, and judicial branches—charged with protecting transparency and ethical governance.[35] Within this framework, archives can be seen as essential infrastructure that enables regulatory bodies to function credibly and substantively. In the absence of a well-maintained archival system, such institutions risk becoming symbolic rather than effective mechanisms of accountability.

## 3.7 Conclusion

This chapter has surveyed the limited but diverse ways in which archives are referenced in national constitutions. While only a small number of constitutions explicitly mention archives, those that do reveal a range of functions, from administrative recordkeeping to the preservation of cultural heritage and foundational legal texts. The typological framework proposed here offers a means to map these references and evaluate their constitutional implications.

The analysis suggests that archives, although often peripheral in constitutional texts, intersect with important constitutional values, including transparency, institutional continuity, and collective memory. Rather than asserting a strong normative claim for the constitutionalization of archives, this chapter has sought to clarify the legal, historical, and symbolic roles that archives already occupy in certain constitutional frameworks. As such, archives should be understood as part of the infrastructural conditions that make constitutional governance possible, even if they are rarely framed as central elements of constitutional design.

Future research might further explore how archival practice interacts with emerging constitutional themes, such as digital governance, transitional justice, and the institutionalization of memory. These inquiries could help refine our understanding of archives not only as repositories of the past but also as enabling conditions for public accountability and constitutional resilience.

## References

Okada J (2021) Archives in parliament: democratic role of the Japanese National Diet Library. In: Fujiyoshi K (ed) Archives for maintaining community and society in the digital age. Springer, p 13

Tushnet M (2021) The new fourth branch: institutions for protecting constitutional democracy. Cambridge University Press

Yokodaido S (2023) Toward diachronic self-government: public records and popular sovereignty in Japan. Keio Online Law J 1:15

[35] *See, e.g.*, Tushnet (2021).

# Chapter 4
# Organizing Local Government Archives in Japan: Current Status and Challenges

**Youhei Jodai**

**Abstract** In this chapter, the history of the creation and development of the concept of "governance archives" in relation to the history of governmental archives in Germany will be clarified. It is important to note that this concept of governance archives, which is intrinsically linked to the fundamental principles of the modern state—namely, democracy and the rule of law—has become a critical infrastructure for state governance. Based on this reasoning, an overview of the status of the development of local government archives will be provided, as evidenced by the results of the Japanese government's survey. It will be demonstrated that there is a current situation in which development is particularly lagging behind in smaller local governments. In light of these conditions, as efforts are made to ensure the functions of governance archives, three strategies will be introduced: the establishment of public record management centers with a focus on the minimum functions of governance archives, the development of joint facilities with similar institutions, and the development of shared facilities with other local governments. The following discussions and considerations will be presented regarding these strategies.

**Keywords** Governance archives · Local autonomy · Self-determination of information · External rules · Functional archival institution

## 4.1 Introduction

This chapter discusses the conditions necessary for the proper functioning of governance archives in local governments in Japan. There are three main points to this chapter. First, it shows that governance archives constitute a fundamental infrastructure of state governance. These archives became necessary with the development of modern states and continue to play a critical role in modern democratic states based

Y. Jodai (✉)
Faculty of Law, Meiji Gakuin University, Tokyo, Japan
e-mail: yojodai@law.meijigakuin.ac.jp



K. Fujiyoshi (ed.), *Governance, Ignorance, and Archives*,
https://doi.org/10.1007/978-981-95-1962-0_4

on the principle of the rule of law. Second, it is important to note that while the state of governance archives in Japan is adequate at the central government and large local government levels, but the proportion of inadequate archives increases as local governments become smaller. Third, measures to ensure the effective functioning of governance archives and to establish related regulations and facilities for local governments in Japan will be proposed. These measures are based on actual examples from some local governments in Japan.

## 4.2 The Concept of "Governance Archives"

Governance archives are defined as mechanisms or facilities for the accumulation and preservation of information related to the governance activities of national and local governments, which are the governing entities. These archives also serve the purpose of disclosing such information to citizens as necessary. In the realm of governance, decision-makers—whether kings and emperors in ancient times or citizens as sovereigns in modern democratic countries—must have access to a plethora of information when making political decisions. Therefore, it is essential for governing activities to preserve information related to governance in a form that can be used.

This concept of governance archives is considered to have originated in the sixteenth-century Germany. At that time, Germany did not yet exist as a modern nation-state, but rather comprised a multitude of smaller states. Each of these states were characterized by the presence of multiple language groups and a variety of regional characteristics. Consequently, effective governance necessitated the collection of essential information, the formulation of political decisions, and the subsequent widespread dissemination of the resulting legislation and ordinances. The necessity of governance archives within the system of governance in these states is precisely demonstrated by this historical precedent. The concept was initially put forth by Jakob von Ramingen von und zu Laiblachsberg, a nobleman and official of the Duchy of Württemberg and the Electorate of the Palatinate. In his book *Von der Registratur / und ihren Gebäwen und Regimenten* (1571), he discussed the necessity of a public document management system for the governance of the state. He pointed out the necessity of establishing archives, which had previously been nothing more than private document repositories for kings, the church, and cloisters, as an institutional framework for the purpose of governing the state. Additionally, he emphasized that the management of documents in such archives for governance must be entrusted to officials who possess a high level of expertise in the administration and politics of the state itself. In the administration of government, it is critical that public documents, which serve as the foundational basis for authority and rights, are perpetually accessible for utilization. Therefore, it is essential that they are preserved and managed in a manner appropriate for that purpose. Consequently, the functions of historical archives, whose mission is to preserve history, and those of governance archives, whose mission is to enable the preservation, management, and use of documents for the administration of government, have become distinct. Subsequent to von Ramingen's formulation of these arguments, each state initiated the accumulation of documents pertaining to governance activities and the attendant authority and rights, thereby independent governance archives were established. These governance archives collected documents selected from the records of the monarch's chambers and privy councils, which were the decision-making bodies of the state at the time. In 1598, in Berlin, Prussia, a system was established whereby the Privy Council Secretary (Kammer Registrator; Archivarius), a senior official, was responsible for the overall management of government documents, and a permanent Privy Archives Office (Geheime Archivskabinett) was set up under the Kammer Registrator. This is considered to be the beginning of governance archives in Germany. This organization contributed to the expansion of Prussian territory and contributed to the collection and organization of official documents from each administrative region, playing a vital role in the expansion and consolidation of Prussian rule. In the nineteenth century, this organization adopted the character and functions of a modern governance archive modeled after the "Haus-, Hof-, und Staatsarchiv (Archives for the house of Habsburg, the Palace of Archduke and the State)" established in Vienna, Austria, in 1749, and was renamed the "Geheimes Staatsarchiv (Privy State Archive)." Following Germany's transition to a republican system of governance in 1919, the establishment of the Reichsarchiv (National archive) in Potsdam as the nation's central public archive occurred. Concurrently, the Geheimes Staatsarchiv relinquished its role as the primary governance archives for the Republic of Germany, while maintaining its function as the governing archive for the state of Prussia and the military.

Governance archives are distinguished from historical archives, which are collections of ancient documents and historical documents, in terms of their function, but the two cannot be completely distinguished from one another. This is because governance activities are the history of a country itself, and history also contains many elements related to governance activities, so it is impossible to clearly distinguish between these two domains. Furthermore, both functions are necessary in order to preserve the history of a country's governance activities. Therefore, it is possible for governance archives to become historical archives over time, and conversely, historical archives may take on the function of governance archives if they are used for governance activities. The Geheimes Staatsarchiv of Prussia lost its function as a governance archive after World War II when the state of Prussia ceased to exist. The Federal Archives in Koblenz, West Germany, and the Central Archives in Potsdam, East Germany, assumed responsibility for its function as a governance archive. The Geheimes Staatsarchiv of Prussia, now a public archive established by the Federal Republic of Germany, serves as a historical archive that houses documents from the former Kingdom of Prussia and the Prussian state, as well as local administrative documents from territories lost by Germany, such as East Prussia and Silesia.

## 4.3 Governance Archives in Modern States

In many modern countries, the government is based on democracy. In a democracy, the people of the country have the power to make decisions regarding the governance of the nation. Consequently, the "freedom to know" as a right to access information constitutes an indispensable foundation for democratic politics, which is predicated on elections conducted through the political decisions of citizens. The dissemination of information related to governance to citizens and its subsequent sharing among them constitutes a fundamental demand of the people as the primary decision-makers in democratic politics. In modern nation states, governance archives can be positioned as one of the key infrastructures of modern democratic states, serving as a mechanism for accumulating, preserving, and disclosing information related to governance activities in response to the freedom to know of citizens.

The German Federal Constitutional Court's 1983 census case judgment (Urteil des Ersten Senats des BVerfG vom 15.12.1983 - 1 BvR 209, 269, 362, 420, 440, 484/83 = BVerfGE 65,1) established the necessity of governance archives in modern states. In this judgment, the Constitutional Court elucidated that the right of citizens to self-determination regarding their personal information is guaranteed as a basic constitutional right, as stated and elaborated as follows:

> anyone who cannot ascertain with sufficient certainty what information relating to them is known in certain areas of their social environment, and anyone who is unable to reasonably assess the knowledge of potential communication partners, may be significantly restricted in their freedom to plan or make decisions based on their own self-determination. ……This would not only impair the individual's opportunities for personal development, but also the common good, because self-determination is a fundamental prerequisite for the functioning of a free and democratic community based on the ability of its citizens to act and participate.

A comparison of the methods of governance employed by democratic states with the content of this judgment reveals two implications for the governance archives of the right to self-determination of information. First, it is imperative to ensure the right to informational self-determination. The public documents related to governance that are the concern of governance archives contain a wide range of personal information. Consequently, national and local public governments, which are responsible for managing public documents, are required to manage these documents in a manner that is appropriate for ensuring the right to self-determination of information. National and local governments must create appropriate documents when carrying out governance activities related to citizens' rights and obligations, and must not only preserve and manage these documents but also ensure their appropriate use and disclosure, while considering data protection. From this perspective, national and local governments have a constitutional obligation to establish systems for the proper preservation and management of public documents, as well as for their disclosure and use where appropriate. Second, the establishment of a public document management system based on external rules. The external rules referred to here correspond to the German term "Rechtssatz" and are understood as rules regarding the rights and obligations of citizens. Under the principle of the rule of law, information self-determination is a basic constitutional right, and therefore any restrictions or specific provisions regarding this right must be based on legal provisions. This means that the authority of governance archives to exercise control over rights to self-determination of information must be granted by external rules, and the existence of such a system also must be based on external rules.

Based on the above implications, between 1987 and 1997, external rules on public document management were enacted in the form of the Public Archives Act (Archivgesetz) in Germany at the federal level and in all 16 federal lands. All governance archives established by the federal government, federal lands, and local governments were positioned as public document management institutions based on these laws, and their authority was clearly defined. Regarding local governance archives, many examples exist where their authority is defined by public records regulations (Archivsatzung) that serve as external rules. All of these laws and regulations place the following three functions at the core of the tasks of governance archives. First, the selection, collection, and acceptance of public documents that should be preserved; second, the appropriate management of important public documents to ensure their permanent preservation; and third, the guarantee of access to public documents for citizens and administrative authorities (e.g., Federal Archives Act §3, Archives Act of the Land of Berlin §3, Archives Regulation of the City of Dresden §4). These three core tasks can be understood as corresponding to the three elements of preservation, management, and utilization that von Ramingen once discussed as essential functions of a governance archive.

## 4.4 Current Situation of Government Archives in Local Public Entities in Japan

During its modernization process in the Meiji Era, Japan mainly adopted the German legal system. The system of governance archives was also introduced to Japan, and in 1885, Naikaku-Bunko (the Cabinet Library) was established as the department responsible for managing Japanese government documents. However, the transfer of governance archives from Germany to Japan was incomplete, and it is considered that the perspective on the use of documents was particularly lacking. In fact, the general use of government documents was not established as a system until after World War II.

The institutionalization of governance archives and the definition of their authority in Japan under external rules was established by the Public Records and Archives Management Act enacted in 2009. According to this Act, public documents of the Japanese government are to be properly preserved and made available for use at the National Archives of Japan, which functions as a governance archive (Article 4, National Archives Act). However, in contrast to Germany, the establishment of

**Table 4.1** Status of Governance Archives in Local Public Governments in Japan (April 2024)

| | | Regional Municipality(47) | | Ordinance-designated city (20) | | other city, town, and village(1721) | |
|---|---|---|---|---|---|---|---|
| | | number | % | number | % | number | % |
| Rules for public document management | Legislated | 47 | 100 | 20 | 100 | 1713 | 99.53 |
| | Within the regulations | 19 | 40.42 | 9 | 45 | 37 | 5.13 |
| | Unlegislated | 0 | 0 | 0 | 0 | 8 | 0.46 |
| Rules for the preservation of public documents | Legislated | 47 | 100 | 19 | 95 | 802 | 46.6 |
| | Unlegislated | 0 | 0 | 1 | 5 | 919 | 53.39 |
| Rules for the utilization of public documents | Legislated | 41 | 87.23 | 12 | 60 | 191 | 11.09 |
| | Unlegislated | 6 | 12.76 | 8 | 40 | 1530 | 88.9 |
| Facilities for public archive | Established | 45 | 95.74 | 14 | 70 | – | – |
| | Within, by the regulations | 29 | 61.7 | 10 | 50 | 52 | 3.02 |
| | Unestablished | 2 | 4.25 | 6 | 30 | – | – |

Source: survey results published by the Cabinet Office on July 26, 2024 [https://www8.cao.go.jp/chosei/koubun/local/mieru/mieru.html]. Table compiled by the author

governance archives by local governments in Japan has not been institutionalized, and their authority has not been clearly defined.

The Cabinet Office of Japan has disclosed the results of a survey on public document management initiatives in local public governments as of April 1, 2024. This survey covered all 47 prefectures, which are Japan's regional municipalities, and 1741 basic municipalities (including 20 government-designated cities). The results of the survey items (1) existence of rules for public document management, (2) existence of rules for the preservation and utilization of public documents preserved as historically valuable, and (3) status of facilities for archiving public documents preserved as historically valuable are summarized in the Table 4.1.

This survey results show that the larger local governments are more advanced in the establishment of governance archives, while smaller local governments are lagging behind in the establishment of systems. According to a 2024 survey, no research has been conducted on the reasons for the lack of progress in the establishment of governance archives by local public governments. Therefore, the causes cannot be clearly identified from this result. According to a 2018 survey conducted by the Japanese government, 60% of basic local governments that do not have public archives and have no plans to establish them cited insufficient resources, such as human resources, financial resources and facilities, as the reason for the lack of progress (Japan Ministry of Internal Affairs and Communications, Survey of 2018. [https://www.soumu.go.jp/main_content/000542521.pdf]). This suggests that the situation may not have changed by 2024.

## 4.5 Approaches to Developing Governance Archives

The following are some examples that may serve as references for local governments in Japan struggling with resource shortages in establishing governance archives.

### *4.5.1 Public Records Management Centers as Alternatives to Public Archives*

In Japan, there is an absence of a formalized system of archivists with the requisite professional competencies and expertise. Consequently, it is uncommon for local governments to engage the services of such specialists. Notwithstanding this, Article 4 of the Archives Act of Japan stipulates that the functions of an archive are to preserve historically important documents and to make them available for public inspection, as well as to carry out research and study on the documents. Securing such specialized staff is particularly problematic for smaller local governments, thus posing a significant obstacle to the establishment of public archives. Consequently, the approach of establishing a governance archive as a public record management center that does not meet the legal standards for a public archive, as outlined in Article 4 of the Public Archives Act, is occasionally employed.

Shimane Prefecture, which enacted the prefectural regulation on public record management in 2011 and established a public record management center in accordance with it, serves as the initial example of such a center (see Fig. 4.1). Shimane Prefecture is one of the least populated and one of the least financially strong of the Regional Municipalities in Japan. Under such conditions, it was difficult for Shimane Prefecture to construct a new archive facility and employ specialist staff. Therefore, Shimane Prefecture decided to re-use the former Prefectural Museum building as a storeroom for historical documents and to establish the public record management center as a system of governance archives focusing on the functions of organizing and preserving documents and making them available to the public.

This method of focusing on only the minimum functions required for governance archives is particularly suitable for smaller municipalities. Other regional municipalities, such as Aomori, Iwate and Yamagata Prefectures, as well as basic municipalities, such as Joetsu City in Niigata Prefecture, have adopted this method.

### *4.5.2 Joint Establishment with Similar Facilities*

In Japan, public awareness of the functions of governance archives is not yet so high, and the development of a stand-alone facility as a public archive is considered unlikely to be a high priority as a use of limited administrative resources. In contrast

**Fig. 4.1** The Shimane Prefectural Public Records Management Center has a designated prefectural government information corner. Users can seamlessly access not only historical documents but also current administrative information. Photo taken by the author in 2022

to the provisions of the Library Act and the Museum Act, the Archives Act does not stipulate conditions regarding the facilities required for public archives. Therefore, archives facilities may be developed in conjunction with other facilities that are easily accessible to the public, such as libraries and museums.

The Ishikawa Prefectural Library is an example of a library that incorporated the function of governance archives into its new facility, which was built in 2022 (see Fig. 4.2). This Library has the highest number of annual users among libraries established by regional governments in Japan, with over one million visitors. Libraries and public archives have the common function of accumulating information and making it available to the public, so this library can fulfil the function of a governance archive. In addition, according to the Library Act, libraries are required to have social education functions and facilities, and to employ professional staff such as librarians, so there is also the advantage that it is easier to secure the expertise that is difficult for public archives to secure on their own.

This method of joint establishment with similar facilities is effective in promoting the utilization of governance archives and is also useful for local governments to broadly disseminate information related to governance. In addition, this method also has the advantage of saving resources such as financial and human resources as compared to establishing public archives separately. The Yamanashi Prefectural Library and Mie Prefectural Museum serve as functions of governance archives. In Haga Town, Tochigi Prefecture, the library, historical museum, and public records office are combined into a single facility called the Information Center.

**Fig. 4.2** The open stacks and reading rooms of the Ishikawa Prefectural Library, which has a hall-like structure. Users can search and use books and public documents across categories. Photo taken by the author in 2023

### *4.5.3 Joint Facilities Operated by Multiple Local Governments*

In Japan, many basic municipalities are facing issues such as a shortage of personal and financial resources. These issues of resource shortage hinder not only the establishment of governance archives but also the development of various public facilities. In such cases, a method traditionally used in Japanese local government is the establishment of joint facilities operated by multiple local governments. In such cases, it has traditionally been common in Japan for multiple local governments to form administrative associations based on the Local Autonomy Act to establish facilities for joint utilization. These association uses contributions from each local government to operate the joint-use facilities.

This method has been commonly used in areas such as schools and hospitals, where financial and staffing burdens tend to be heavy, and is also suitable for the establishment of governance archives. In fact, in Germany, where a similar system of municipal associations (Gemeindeverband) exists, this method is commonly used to establish municipal archive facilities. However, local authorities in Japan generally take a cautious or negative stance toward entrusting the management of public documents to associations outside the local government. Therefore, this method has not yet become common practice for local governance archives.

**Fig. 4.3** The Fukuoka Communal Archives is located in Chikushino City in the central part of the prefecture, established as a combined facility of the Fukuoka Prefectural Archive and the Municipal Archives. Photo by the author in 2015

The Fukuoka Communal Archives (see Fig. 4.3) is a public archive facility operated by an administrative association of Fukuoka Prefecture and basic municipalities within the prefecture (excluding government-designated cities). Historically important documents owned by basic municipalities within the prefecture are preserved and managed by communal archives and made available for use by citizens at communal archives. This method has the advantage of reducing the burden on individual basic municipalities compared to establishing their own public archive facilities, while also ensuring the functions of governance archives are adequately fulfilled. However, municipalities located far from communal archives may be concerned that even their own documents will be difficult for the authorities and citizens to access there. Consequently, when adopting this method, it is imperative to consider measures that will guarantee access to the documents.

## 4.6 Overview

The functions of governance archives are essential in modern democratic states under the principle of the rule of law, and these functions must be ensured not only at the national level but also at the local government level. It is a fact that, depending on the regional characteristics, scale, and circumstances of local governments, it may be difficult to ensure the functions of governance archives. However, as in Germany, where the concept of a "functional archival institution" emerged and legal measures were proposed to address such challenges, efforts to ensure the functions of governance archives in Japan should also be closely monitored.

There are several issues to consider regarding the development of governance archives. First, there is the financial issue. The Archives Act of Japan stipulates in Article 6 that "the national government shall endeavor to provide financial assistance or mediation to local governments for the establishment of archives," but in reality, governance archives are facilities established by local governments to preserve, manage, and make public their own official documents. Therefore, the financial burden for their establishment and operation generally falls on the local governments themselves. If this financial burden hinders the development of governance archives at local levels, it is necessary to reconsider the rationale behind the provision of Article 6 of the Archives Act. Second, there is the issue of standardizing the functions of governance archives. The necessity of how to organize governance archives and ensure their functions varies across local governments nationwide. As there is no standardized approach, each local government is currently experimenting with different methods. Article 7 of the Archives Act authorizes the Prime Minister to provide technical guidance or advice to local governments regarding the operation of their public archives. Therefore, the means to utilize the specialized expertise of National Archives, such as the public records management support (Archivpflege) stipulated in German Archives Act, should also be considered.

The development of democracy and the realization of the rule of law depend on the functioning of governance archives. This chapter aims to contribute to the ongoing discussion on ensuring the functioning of governance archives at the local government level.

## References

### *Japanese*

Hayakawa K (2022) Public records and archives management act and local government. In: Miyama J (ed) Local governments and document management in the age of the public records and archives management act (kōbunsho kanrihō jidai no jititai to bunsyo kanri). Bensei Syuppan, pp 23–48

Hayakawa K (eds) Study Group on Local Public Document Management Regulations (2019) In such circumstances, what course of action should be taken? The management of documentation by local government (Konna Toki Dōsuru?—Jichitai no Kōbunsyo Kanri). Dai-Ichi Hōki

Ikebata C (2022) Opening of the Ishikawa Prefectural Library (Ishikawa kenritsu Tosyokan no kaikan ni tsuite). Archives (Web J Natl Archiv) 86. https://www.archives.go.jp/publication/archives/no086/12761

Iwasaki K (2015) Opening of the Shimane Prefectural Public Document Center (Shimane ken Kōbunsyo Sentā no kaikan ni tsuite). Archives (Natl Archiv) 47:37–39

Jodai Y (2014) The systemic principle of archive. In: Jodai Y (ed) Essencials of the archival sciences (ākaibuzugaku yōron). Shogakusya, pp 60–93

Kato K (2024) Social contribution through archives. In: The National Institute of Japanese Literature (ed) Introduction to archival sciences (ākaibuzugaku nyūmon), pp 161–175. Benseisya

Kohara Y (2015) About the opening of the Fukuoka Communal Archives and its initiatives (Fukuoka Kyōdō Kōbunsyokan no kaikan to sono torikumi ni tsuite). Archives 49:1–8

### *English, German*

Berger H (2019) Öffentliche Archive und staatliches Wissen. Techtum

Brenneke A (1953) Archivkunde: Ein Beitrag zur Theorie und Geschichte des Europäischen Archivwesens. Koeler & Amelang (Bearb. v. LEESCH, W. Rep. De Gruyter, 1988)

Franz EG, Lux T (2018) Einführung in die Archivkunde, 9th edn. Wissenschaftliche Buchgesellschaft

Jodai Y (2025) Introducing the concept of a "functional archival institution": promoting public records management administration in local governments in Japan. Musashino Hogaku (Musashino University) 22:27(219)–42(204)

Lütteken A (2016) Aufklärung und Historisumus. In: Lepper M, Raulff U (eds) Handbuch Archiv S. 45–56. J.B. Metzler

Manegold B (2001) Archivrecht: Die Archivierungspflicht öffentlicher Stellen und das Archivzugangsrecht des historischen Forschers im Licht der Forschungsfreiheitsverbürgung des Art. 5 Abs. 3 GG. Duncker & Humblot

Oegg JA (1804) Ideen einer Theorie der Archivwissenschaft. C.W. Ettinger (Rep. Wentworth Press, 2015)

Schreyer H (2008) Das staatliche Archivwesen der DDR: Ein Überblick. Droste Verlag

Staub M (2016) Mittelalter und Frühe Neuzeit. In: Lepper M, Raulff U (eds) Handbuch Archiv S. 40–44. J.B. Metzler

Weiß PU (2022) Deutsche Zentralarchive in den Systemumbrüchen nach 1933 und 1945. Wallstein

# Chapter 5
# Immigration and Records Management in Japan

**Misako Fukushima**

**Abstract** This chapter analyzes how immigration records are kept in Japan, examining who maintains them and under what policies. Then, it investigates the rationale behind current record-keeping methods and identifies any associated issues. Finally, it assesses the future of immigrant record management in contemporary Japan. According to the findings, Japan's immigration records have historically relied on official statistics and policy documents due to the official stance that "there are no immigrants" and a vertically divided administrative structure, resulting in challenges in continuity and permanent preservation. The chapter concludes by emphasizing the importance of immigration policy, a multi-layered approach to records, and promoting greater access to and utilization of these vital documents.

**Keywords** Immigration policy · Records management · Foreign labor · Foreign student · No immigrants in Japan

## 5.1 Setting the Context: Immigration Policy and Record Management

According to the International Organization for Migration (IOM), the number of international migrants is on the rise, reaching 281 million in 2020 (IOM website). This accounts for approximately 3.6% of the world's population. In Japan, as of the end of June 2024, the number of foreign residents had reached a record high of 3,588,956 (Immigration Services Agency of Japan 2024).

As a researcher of immigration policy, investigating and analyzing what policies incentivize or hinder the process of foreigners entering Japan, learning, working, and eventually settling there, I aim in this chapter to examine whether, and if so how, such immigrant records are managed, and what impact this has on policy.

M. Fukushima (✉)
Bureau of Human Empowerment, University of Tsukuba, Tsukuba, Japan
e-mail: fukushima.misako.fp@u.tsukuba.ac.jp



K. Fujiyoshi (ed.), *Governance, Ignorance, and Archives*,
https://doi.org/10.1007/978-981-95-1962-0_5

By the way, to whom are we referring when we say "migrants"? In fact, unlike "refugees" under international law, there is no clear definition. However, the United Nations (UN) defines migrants as follows:

> While there is no formal legal definition of an international migrant, most experts agree that an international migrant is someone who changes his or her country of usual residence, irrespective of the reason for migration or legal status. Generally, a distinction is made between short-term or temporary migration, covering movements with a duration between three and 12 months, and long-term or permanent migration, referring to a change of country of residence for a duration of one year or more. (UN website)

Therefore, in this chapter as well, I define those who reside for 12 months or more as long-term migrants, and those who reside for 3–12 months as short-term migrants.

This chapter first clarifies how the record management of immigrants in Japan is analyzed by summarizing previous studies on international migration and its records. Next, it reviews the history of Japanese policies regarding the acceptance of foreign workers and students and clarifies how and why these people entered Japan. Among the types of legal migrants covered by the IOM are migrant workers who belong to a clearly defined legal category, and international students whose status and means of movement are not clearly defined in international law (IOM website). Therefore, it is considered necessary to focus on these two types. Based on this, I analyze who is keeping records and how under such policies, including the possibility that no records are being kept. Then, I examine why such record-keeping methods are being used and whether there are any problems with these methods. Finally, I summarize the prospects for immigrant record management in the present-day Japan.

## 5.2 Literature Review

### *5.2.1 Prior Research on International Migration Studies*

In recent years, the study of international migration has increased in importance and diversity, and its complexity is being explored from various perspectives. This chapter organizes the main discussions and results of previous studies.

Massey et al. (1993) comprehensively reviewed and evaluated the main theories in international migration studies. By analyzing in detail the six theories of neoclassical economics, new economics, world systems theory, network theory, institutional theory, and cumulative causation, and examining how each theory explains the occurrence, continuation, and patterns of international migration, they provided a theoretical framework for understanding the complex phenomenon of international migration and laid the foundation for policy formulation and further research. In particular, they emphasized the importance of comprehensively analyzing macro-level and micro-level factors, as well as the roles of social networks and institutions.

*The Age of Migration* by Castles and Miller (1993) is an early study on international migration that presents the basic concepts and theoretical framework of population movement. Based on an analysis of the historical background and contemporary characteristics of international population movement, it provides a comprehensive consideration of various forms of movement, such as that of immigrants, refugees, and foreign workers and presents a theoretical framework for the impact of population movement on the state, economy, and society, clarifying its complex dynamics in the modern era. In particular, it discusses how economic factors and political trends have influenced the flow of immigrants, providing an important perspective for understanding the role of immigrants in the process of global integration. Vertovec and Cohen (2003), whose work succeeded this book, analyzed the increasing complexity and diversification of population movement due to the progress of globalization and raised new challenges in modern society. Specifically, these include the integration of immigrants, multiculturalism, and citizenship. They used concepts that were new at that time for their analysis, such as superdiversity and transnationalism.

Zolberg (1981) focuses on both economic and political factors. He also emphasizes the fact that international cooperation is indispensable for formulating effective immigration policies. Furthermore, he lists the balance between national sovereignty and international cooperation, immigrant integration, and human rights protection as issues of modern immigration policy (Zolberg 1989). Arendt (2007), based on her own experience, focuses on the marginality of life faced by international migrants and considers the legal status of exile and immigrants.

As is clear from the above prior research, international migration research provides an important framework for comprehensively understanding the social, economic, and political impacts of immigrants, beyond the mere analysis of population movement.

### *5.2.2 Prior Research on International Migration Records: From the Perspective of Oral History and Immigrant Archives*

The history of immigrants, which requires a comprehensive understanding of their social, economic, and political impacts, encompasses multilayered experiences and meanings that cannot be captured by mere statistics and official records. Therefore, how to record, preserve, and share the immigrant experience with society is an important issue.

Sommer (2006) discusses in detail the role that oral history plays in the formation of public memory. She points out that individual testimonies are not merely private records, but have the power to complement and sometimes revise the historical understanding of society as a whole. In the history of immigrants, in particular, individual experiences that are not recorded in official records have a great impact on the formation of communities and the maintenance of identity.

In Japan, the experiences of overseas immigrants before and after World War II (e.g., Brazilian immigrants and Japanese-American immigrants) and the increasing number of foreign workers in recent years cannot be fully understood by official statistics alone. Oral history complements such insufficient materials. For example, the adaptation process of Japanese-Brazilians in Japanese society and the working environment of technical intern trainees are important issues that are revealed through oral history for the first time. Collecting these individual voices can contribute to the evaluation of Japanese immigration policies and the practice of multicultural coexistence. For example, Sakugawa et al. (2019) uncovered the pride and values of first-generation elderly Okinawan-Bolivian immigrants from their narratives and obtained suggestions for regional care systems that consider the culture of the place of immigration. Also, Kikuchi and Tsutsumi (2021) listened to whether Okinawans who immigrated from Okinawa to Brazil were able to pass on their daily meals from their hometown at home in their immigration destination. On the other hand, there are not many studies of oral history on foreigners who have immigrated to Japan.

Furthermore, while Chung (2021) empirically demonstrated the mechanism by which the occupational status of Koreans in Japan diverges into three categories, namely, economic assimilation, ethnic economization, and underclass formation, even though more than 30 years have passed since newcomers came to Japan, research still predominantly focuses on oldcomers. The political background whereby the government publicly recognizes "immigrants" only as immigrants from Japan to overseas, which will be mentioned later, may also have an influence.

In immigrant records, archives are as important as oral history. While oral history is a record based on personal spontaneous statements, archives include records that the person themselves may not be aware of leaving. Consequently, Soysal (2021) discusses the political and social significance of immigrant records. She points out that such records are not merely a preservation of the past, but influence the policies and identity formation of modern society. In particular, because immigrant records often have "transnational" characteristics that transcend national frameworks, they may not be fully positioned within a country's national history. In Japan, the development of immigrant archives is still in its infancy. For example, public records of Japanese immigrants before the war are fragmentary, lacking details, in particular, of individual migration experiences and lives. Furthermore, even though Japan became an "immigrant-receiving country" following the period of economic growth after the war, its records are often confined within institutional frameworks, and the perspectives of the immigrants themselves are often not sufficiently reflected. Soysal's research suggests the need for multilayering and expanding access to immigrant records in Japan. A more comprehensive immigrant archive can be formed by developing a system that allows immigrant communities to record and disseminate their own experiences, in addition to public immigrant data.

## 5.3 Immigration History in Japan

Immigration management in Japan regulates the entry and residency of foreign nationals, thereby influencing the nation's workforce, political stability, and socio-economic landscape. This section examines Japan's immigration history, focusing on the acceptance of foreign laborers and students.

### *5.3.1 Evolution of Foreign Labor Acceptance*

The evolution of Japan's immigration control system can be categorized into three distinct periods: "Meiji era to World War II (1899–1945)," "post–World War II to 1990 (1945–1990)," and "1990 onwards." While limited foreign entry occurred before 1899, this analysis concentrates on the period following the establishment of formal residency management.

#### Meiji Era to World War II (1899–1945)

Japan's immigration management originated during the Meiji era, following a prolonged period of national isolation. According to Akashi (2010), the "Overseas Passport Regulations" (Ministry of Foreign Affairs [MOFA] 1878), the Foreign Ministry's initial edict, served as the precursor to the modern Passport Act. This regulation mandated passports as proof of nationality and visas for legal departure and entry. The foundation of Japan's immigration and residency management was laid in 1899 with the abolition of segregated foreign residential areas, allowing for "mixed residency" (Akashi 2010, pp. 62–63). The global escalation of border controls during World War I prompted Japan to enact the Ministry of Interior Ordinance No. 1, "Regarding Foreigners Entering Japan" in 1918 (Ministry of Home Affairs 1918), which constituted Japan's first comprehensive immigration law.

#### Post–World War II to 1990 (1945–1990)

From the end of World War II until the enforcement of the San Francisco Peace Treaty with the Allied Nations in 1952, the General Headquarters (GHQ) of the Allied Forces in Japan directed Japan's immigration control. This period witnessed the centralization of immigration management, consolidating various responsibilities previously dispersed among different ministries. In 1950, the Immigration Bureau was established within the MOFA, integrating functions such as regular immigration, foreigner registration, and enforcement against illegal entry. Subsequently, in 1952, the Immigration Bureau, renamed the Immigration Control Agency, was transferred to the Ministry of Justice [MOJ], where it remains today.

While industrialized nations like the United States and those in western Europe relied on immigrant labor during their industrialization (Doeringer and Piore 1971), Japan's post-World War II economic growth was primarily fueled by domestic seasonal workers (Sassen 2001). Consequently, residency management focused on "oldcomers" who had lost Japanese nationality due to the San Francisco Peace Treaty in 1951.

#### 1990 Onwards

The 1990 amendment of the Immigration Control Act marked a significant shift. As Japan's "bubble economy" faced labor shortages, companies turned to foreign laborers. Recruitment agencies facilitated the entry of Japanese descendants from Latin America, particularly Japanese-Brazilians, as family visitors (Ninomiya 2014, pp. 343–344). This led to the rapid establishment of "settler" status to accommodate these individuals.

The 1990 amendment also influenced the acceptance of foreign knowledge workers. Amid the global IT boom of the late 1990s, Japan sought to revitalize its economy by attracting foreign IT engineers. Prime Minister Yoshiro Mori's 2000 visit to India and the subsequent "Japan–India IT Cooperation Promotion Plan" (Akashi 2010, pp. 155–156) exemplified this policy. In 2012, the MOJ's Immigration Bureau introduced the "Point-based Preferential Immigration Control System for Highly Skilled Foreigners" to facilitate the entry of highly skilled professionals.

As of 2024, approximately 2.3 million of Japan's 3.5 million foreign residents are employed, out of a total population of 123 million (Immigration Services Agency of Japan 2024; Ministry of Health, Labour, and Welfare [MHLW] 2025) (Fig. 5.1).

### *5.3.2 Evolution of Japan's Foreign Student Acceptance Policy*

This section examines the historical evolution of Japan's foreign student acceptance policy from World War II to the present, identifying key policies that have shaped its development. The objectives of these policies can be categorized into three primary areas: (1) political and diplomatic strategy; (2) academic and cultural international exchange; and (3) economic and highly skilled talent acquisition. Japan's postwar foreign student acceptance policy has transitioned through these stages, evolving from a focus on political and diplomatic objectives to academic and international exchange, and ultimately to economic and highly skilled talent acquisition.

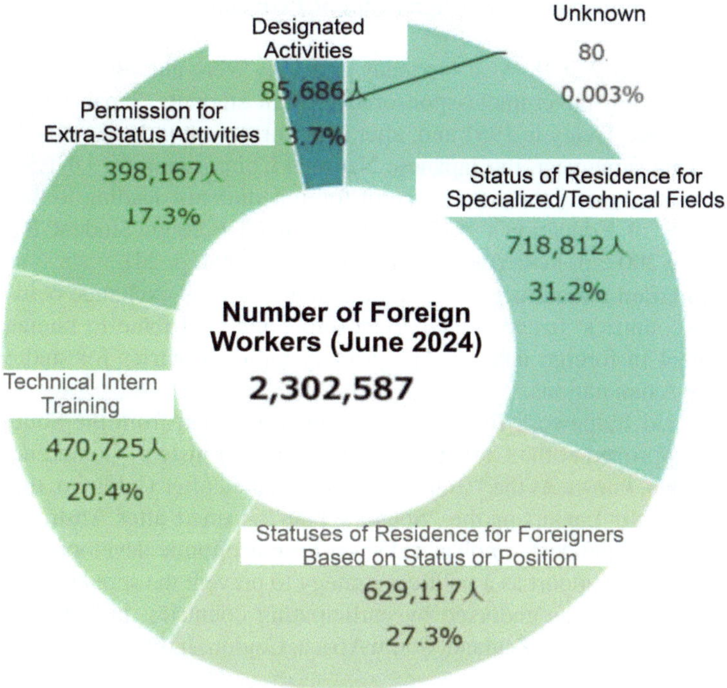


**Fig. 5.1** Number of Foreign Workers. *Source*: MHLW (2025)

## The Southern Special Foreign Student Program

Toward the end of World War II, as part of Prime Minister Hideki Tojo's Greater East Asia Co-Prosperity Sphere initiative, Japan, invited 205 students from various occupied territories in Southeast Asia as government-sponsored students. This initiative, formally known as the "Education and Training Program for Special Southern Cultural Leaders" and commonly referred to as the "Southern Special Foreign Student Program," was overseen by the MOFA under the Greater East Asia Ministry, established in 1943. The International Student Institute Association, a foundation under the Foreign Ministry, managed the program (Horie 2002, p. 322; Takeda 2006, p. 82).

The primary objective of this program was to cultivate future leaders from occupied territories who would cooperate with Japan, facilitating smoother colonial administration. Many of the students were children of influential figures in their respective regions, who were expected to play key roles in the future (Yoh 2014, p. 57). The primary purpose of the program was rooted in (1) political and diplomatic strategy.

## The Government-Funded Foreign Student Program

Following World War II, West Germany and Italy were among the first nations to resume accepting government-sponsored foreign students. Japan signed the San Francisco Peace Treaty in 1951 and, after its enforcement in 1952, joined UNESCO in 1953. That same year, the Japanese National Commission for UNESCO recommended strengthening the acceptance of foreign students, leading to the launch of the Ministry of Education's "Government-Funded Foreign Student Program" in 1954 (Horie 2002, p. 324; Yokota and Shiratsuchi 2004, p. 24).

This program aimed to promote international cultural exchange between Japan and other countries, foster mutual friendships, and contribute to human resource development in foreign nations. The primary target countries for student recruitment were Asian nations.

Japan's aid framework for Asian countries originated from the Southeast Asia Aid Plan, approved at the Commonwealth Foreign Ministers' Conference in 1950. This initiative, known as the "Colombo Plan" (named after Colombo, the capital of Ceylon, now Sri Lanka) or the "Spender Plan" (named after Australian Foreign Minister Percy Spender), emphasized short-term economic development and long-term educational support as a political strategy to prevent the spread of communism in Asia. The plan was endorsed by participating countries, including the United Kingdom, Canada, New Zealand, South Africa, Ceylon, India, and Pakistan (Takeda 1991, pp. 124–125).

Japan joined the Colombo Plan in 1954, indicating that the primary purpose of its foreign student policy at the time was (1) political and diplomatic strategy, although elements of (2) academic and international exchange were also present.

## The 100,000 Foreign Students Plan

In 1983, under the directive of Prime Minister Yasuhiro Nakasone, the "100,000 Foreign Students Plan" was launched (Ministry of Education, Culture, Sports, Science, and Technology [MEXT] 2001). The background to this lies in Japan's rapid economic growth during the 1980s. While this growth heightened awareness of Japan's international status and role, the increasing economic friction between Japan and other countries led to a rise in anti-Japanese sentiment, particularly in the business sector. This, in turn, created a growing recognition of the need for international human exchange (Horie 2002, pp. 83–84; Takeda 2006, p. 83). The policy strongly reflected the goal of (2) academic and cultural international exchange.

## The 300,000 Foreign Students Plan

Having achieved the 100,000-student target by 2003, the administration of Prime Minister Yasuo Fukuda (2007–2008) formulated and implemented the "300,000 Foreign Students Plan." This plan aimed to expand the acceptance of talented foreign students in collaboration with industry, academia, and government, facilitating their entry into graduate programs and employment in Japanese companies (Prime Minister's Office 2008). The policy framework was jointly developed by the MEXT, the MOFA, the MOJ, the MHLW, the Ministry of Economy, Trade and Industry, and the Ministry of Land, Infrastructure, Transport, and Tourism. This demonstrated that Japan's foreign student policy had evolved beyond being solely an educational policy managed by the MEXT (MEXT et al. 2008).

The "300,000 Foreign Students Plan" adopted a comprehensive approach, taking into consideration foreign students' entire journey—from recruitment before arrival to their employment and settlement in Japanese society after graduation.

The "global competition for talent" has intensified, and countries are actively recruiting highly skilled individuals and encouraging them to stay in their countries after studying to contribute to their economies. The "300,000 Foreign Students Plan" also adopted a comprehensive approach, considering the entire process from pre-arrival recruitment to employment and settlement in Japanese society after graduation, aiming for the settlement of highly skilled talent in Japan. As a result, the "300,000 Foreign Students Plan" was not merely an expansion of the previous "100,000 Foreign Students Plan" but marked a significant shift from a mutual benefit model to an economy-driven model. In other words, Japan transitioned from (2) academic and cultural international exchange to (3) economic and highly skilled talent acquisition.

Although the number of foreign students decreased due to the impact of COVID-19, the Japanese government pursued its goal of attracting 300,000 foreign students, successfully reaching this target in 2019 (Fig. 5.2).

## Toward "400,000 Foreign Students"

Following the achievement of the "300,000 Foreign Students Plan," the Kishida Fumio Cabinet (2021–2023) announced a plan to increase the number of Japanese students studying abroad to 500,000 and to accept and retain 400,000 foreign students in Japan by 2033 (Council for the Creation of Future Education 2023). Similarly to the MEXT's selection of 13 universities for the "Promotion of Forming University Internationalization Networks" project from AY2009–2013 and 27 universities for the "Top Global University Project" from AY2014–2023 (13 Type A: Top Global Universities, 24 Type B: Global Traction Universities) in line with the 300,000 Foreign Students Plan, the ministry aims to promote the internationalization of all universities in Japan by disseminating successful case studies nationwide through the selection of 13 universities for the "Support Project for Creating Social Impact Through University Internationalization" from AY2024–2029 (10 Type I: Regional Collaboration Universities, 3 Type II: Overseas Development Universities) to advance the 400,000 student plan.

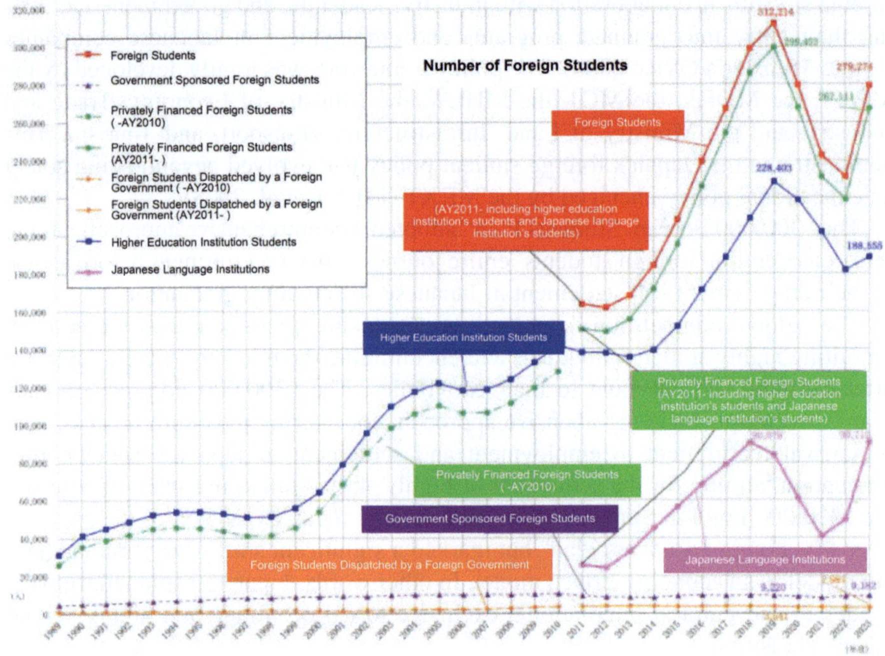


Fig. 5.2 Number of Foreign Students. *Source*: Japan Student Services Organization (2024)

## 5.3.3 "There Are No Immigrants in Japan"

As described above, Japan is already accepting immigrants. However, despite having over 2.3 million foreign workers and more than 300,000 international students, Japan maintains that "there are no immigrants in Japan." There are two reasons for this.

First, the term "immigrant" has a politically negative connotation in Japan. Until World War II, Japan colonized Taiwan and Korea, and granted their residents Japanese nationality. However, after the war, Japan relinquished its colonies, and these people were stripped of their Japanese nationality. The Alien Registration System, which required foreign residents in Japan to register their place of residence and personal information with municipalities, was enacted during the post–World War II turmoil to grasp and manage the situation of these denationalized foreign residents. It was established as the "Alien Registration Ordinance" in 1947 and later legalized as the "Alien Registration Act" in 1952. Those managed under this system faced social discrimination.

Unlike European countries, such as Germany, which accepted foreign workers from Turkey and elsewhere for postwar reconstruction, Japan relied on manual laborers from rural Japan (Sassen 2001). Consequently, until the 1990 amendment of the Immigration Control and Refugee Recognition Act, the term "foreigners" primarily referred to "oldcomers" who had migrated from Taiwan and Korea and continued to reside in Japan after losing their nationality. As a result, "immigrants" came to mean Japanese emigrants to Hawaii, the United States mainland, and South America from the nineteenth to the twentieth century—that is, immigrants as senders.

On the other hand, as a receiving country, the term came into use after the 1990 amendment of the Immigration Control and Refugee Recognition Act. However, the reason for this amendment was to accept Japanese immigrants from South America as blue-collar workers, not with the intention of permanent residency. This was a "reception system for foreign workers through a rotation system or a circulation policy, accepting foreign workers for a short period while preventing them from settling permanently" (Kamibayashi 2015). Consequently, they were not only regarded as "short-term residents" but also contributed to the negative image of immigrants.

Second, Japan lacks a legal concept of immigrants. Therefore, in response to requests and questions at the House of Representatives such as, "Please provide the government's definition of 'immigrants' and 'immigration policy' in our country," "Please provide the reasons why the Abe Cabinet has 'no intention of adopting so-called immigration policies,'" and "Do you recognize that foreign workers include immigrants?" the government replied, "The terms 'immigrants' and 'immigration policies' are used in various contexts, and it is difficult to give a general answer regarding their definitions and the foreign workers you mentioned." With regard to the question of "Is it legally possible for administrations other than the Abe Cabinet to adopt 'so-called immigration policies' under the current law?" the government stated, "It is difficult to answer because the specific meaning of 'so-called immigration policies' is unclear" (House of Representatives 2018a, b). It seems that the government is avoiding using the term "immigrants" in public and responding cautiously.

As the definition of immigrants is not clarified, there is no need for a legal framework. Consequently, the government does not need to consider who falls into which legal category. Therefore, the argument that there is no need to monitor or manage immigrants and that there is no ministry for that purpose becomes valid.

In recent years, due to the increased number of foreign workers in Japan and the labor shortage accompanying the declining population, the importance of immigration policy has risen, and some politicians and experts have called for the establishment of an "Immigration Agency" to specialize in an immigration policy. The main purposes of establishing an Immigration Agency include the unification and efficiency of immigration policies, the development of a system for accepting foreign workers, and the realization of a multicultural society. However, there is no movement within the Japanese government to establish an Immigration Agency.

## 5.4 Conclusion and Discussion

### 5.4.1 Conclusion: The Fragmented Landscape of Immigration Records

The Foreigner Registration System based on the "Alien Registration Act" in 1952 was abolished with the 2009 amendment of the Immigration Control and Refugee Recognition Act. Part of the background to this was the criticism from foreigners, mainly oldcomers, regarding the human rights issues of the system, such as the mandatory fingerprinting. With the residence management system newly introduced with the abolition of this registration system, foreign nationals are now required to report changes of address, and their affiliated organizations are also required to report. As a result, "the Minister of Justice has become able to grasp the residence status of the foreign national more accurately and continuously than before" (MOJ 2012).

Thus, in the current situation, the MOJ has become able to manage where foreign nationals, including immigrants, reside and to which organizations they belong. However, based on the following definition from archives, it is believed that the residence management system cannot be called an archive of immigrants.

> A collection or body of records created, received, used and kept by an individual, family, corporation, government or other public or private organization in the course of its activities, whether analog or digital and regardless of medium, and preserved permanently by itself or its legal successor for the continuous value as evidence, information and assets of its activities and events. (Archival Terminology Research Society 2024)

The major reason it is not considered an archive is the lack of continuity and permanent preservation by a legal successor. In Japan, where there is no centralized authority for immigration oversight, the management of immigration records is distributed across multiple ministries. The Immigration Services Agency, under the MOJ, handles immigration control. The MEXT manages records pertaining to international students, while the MHLW is responsible for labor-related data (Fig. 5.3). Consequently, a comprehensive institution for the long-term recording and management of immigration data is lacking.

Furthermore, the data held by each ministry are predominantly quantitative. Qualitative data, conversely, are managed by disparate entities. For instance, records

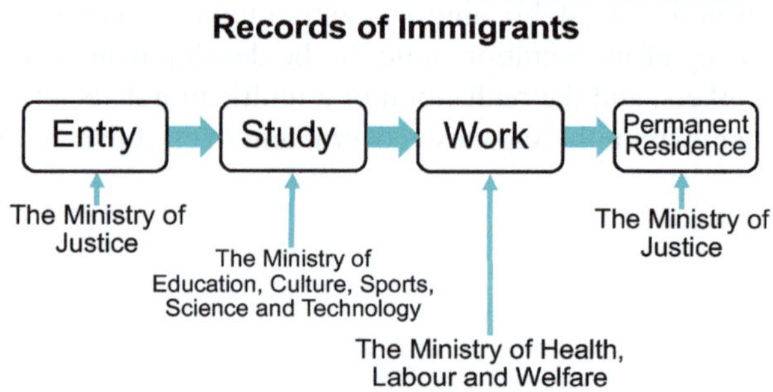


**Fig. 5.3** Records of Immigrants. Note: Created by the author

of Japanese emigrants to South America are housed at the Japanese Overseas Migration Museum, operated by the Japan International Cooperation Agency (JICA), an affiliate of the MOFA. Similarly, historical records of Korean residents in Japan (oldcomers) are maintained by the History Museum of Korean Residents in Japan, managed by the Korean Residents Union in Japan (Mindan). Thus, qualitative data on immigrants in Japan largely rely on records from sending countries or private immigrant communities.

### *5.4.2 Discussion*

Why does no one try to take responsibility for the long-term impact? There are two reasons. First, it relies on the absence of a legal concept of immigrants. As a result, the Japanese government does not need to monitor or manage immigrants. Second, Japan's excessively vertically divided bureaucracy, where many ministries handle individual issues, leads to a lack of coordination and a tendency to prioritize short-term gains over long-term plans and strategies.

Isn't the lack of a legal concept of immigrants and immigration control due to excessive inefficient bureaucracy, without a long-term perspective? Surprisingly, it seems to be functioning in its current state. This is because, under the current residence management system, reporting by affiliated organizations is also mandatory, and immigrants cannot maintain their residence status without a sponsor. For example, international students can enter Japan and maintain their residence status because educational institutions act as sponsors. Students who drop out of school must return to their home countries. The same applies to workers. With some exceptions, generally, even highly skilled foreigners cannot enter Japan without a sponsoring company. As a result, foreigners have to return home upon losing their jobs. Therefore, the government can track immigrants if it tracks sponsors. Of course, it is impossible to track those who disappear after dropping out or resigning and become illegal immigrants.

It may seem that there are no obstacles to immigration control at present. However, the inability to create long-term immigration records is problematic in many ways. First, due to the lack of continuity, the Japanese government cannot have comprehensive responsibility and a full understanding of immigration issues. Even if fragmented records are collected from each ministry, only fragmented facts can be obtained. As a result, the Japanese government continues to assert that there are no immigrants and avoids establishing a coherent immigration policy. Second, there is a lack of permanent preservation by a legal successor. Due to the lack of continuity, there is also a lack of continuity regarding preservation, and as a result, permanent preservation becomes impossible. Furthermore, the ambiguity of regulations regarding the disposal of records damages administrative accountability and transparency, as well as the public's right to know. Third, the lack of a perspective on the preservation and inheritance of historical and cultural values, and the contribution to academic research and education, neglects the contribution to society.

## 5.5 Implication: Future Prospects for Immigration Records Management

While facing issues with continuity and permanent preservation, Japan's immigration records have traditionally relied on official statistics and policy documents. To compensate for these shortcomings, integrating perspectives from oral history and immigrant archives would enable a more comprehensive understanding of immigration history. As Sommer (2006) suggests, incorporating the individual voices of immigrants into the public memory is crucial for fostering acceptance and coexistence within Japanese society. Furthermore, Soysal (2021) argues that immigration records are not merely historical artifacts but also shape current and future immigration policies and identity formation.

Based on these scholarly insights, three key considerations emerge for addressing the challenges and potential improvements in Japan's immigration records. First, there is an immigration policy. By defining immigrants, we can take a step toward continuously recording and storing immigrant records. At the same time, regardless of immigration, regulations concerning the disposal of records should be established, and a system for permanent preservation should also be put in place. Second, there is a multilayered approach to immigration records. This includes integrating official data with voluntary community records and materials collected by NGOs and research institutions to create archives that reflect diverse perspectives. The systematic collection and preservation of oral histories is also crucial. Documenting the experiences of immigrants, from pre- and postwar emigrants to contemporary international students, would provide valuable resources for shaping future immigration policies. Third, promoting access to and the utilization of immigration records is important. Developing platforms that facilitate easy access to immigrant histories and experiences for both the general public and policymakers, such as interactive digital archives and the integration of migration history into educational curricula, is essential. This will enhance the recognition of the importance of archives, not only for record management and preservation but also for documentation.

## References

Akashi J (2010) Japan's immigration control policy: foundation and transition. Nakanishiya Shuppan. [AZ-631-J32]

Archival Terminology Research Society. (2024). Dictionary of archival science. Kashiwa Shobo. [UL2-R4]

Arendt H (2007) In: Braumuller S (ed) Exiled in America: life on the margins in a global world. Schocken Books

Castles S, Miller MJ (1993) The age of migration: international population movements in the modern world. Guilford Press

Chung K (2021) The contemporary mechanism of occupational status attainment by Zainichi Koreans: economic assimilation, ethnic enclavization and underclassization. Soshioroji 65(3):21–38. [Z6-262]

Council for the Creation of Future Education (2023, April 27) Japan - mobility and internationalisation: Re-engaging and accelerating initiative for future generations (J-MIRAI) outline. https://www.cas.go.jp/jp/seisaku/kyouikumirai/pdf/230427outline.pdf. Accessed 25 Mar 2025

Doeringer PB, Piore MJ (1971) International labor markets and manpower analysis: with a new introduction. M. E. Sharpe

Horie M (2002) Horon Nihon no ryugakusei ukeire seisaku no suii (appendix the transition of Japan's international student acceptance policy). In: Kaku K, Hirano K (eds) 21 seiki no kokusai chiteki koryu to Nihon: Nichi-Bei Furuburaito 50 nen o fumaete (International intellectual exchange and Japan in the 21st century: based on 50 years of the Japan-U.S. Fulbright program). Chuo Koron Shinsha [FD43-H19], pp 322–343

House of Representatives (Shugiin) (2018a) Inquiry concerning foreign workers and immigration (Question No. 104, 196th Session of the Diet). https://www.shugiin.go.jp/internet/itdb_shitsumon_pdf_s.nsf/html/shitsumon/pdfS/a196104.pdf/$File/a196104.pdf. Accessed 15 Apr 2025

House of Representatives (Shugiin) (2018b) Answer to the inquiry concerning foreign workers and immigration (Answer No. 104, 196th Session of the Diet). https://www.shugiin.go.jp/internet/itdb_shitsumon_pdf_t.nsf/html/shitsumon/pdfT/b196104.pdf. Accessed 15 Apr 2025

Immigration Services Agency of Japan (2024) The number of foreign residents in Japan as of the end of June 2024. https://www.moj.go.jp/isa/publications/press/13_00047.html. Accessed 15 Apr 2025

International Organization for Migration (n.d.) Who is a migrant? https://www.iom.int/who-migrant. Accessed 25 Mar 2025

Japan Student Services Organization (JASSO) (2024) Results of the 2023 (Reiwa 5) Survey on the status of international students. https://www.studyinjapan.go.jp/ja/statistics/enrollment/data/2405241100.html. Accessed 15 Apr 2025

Kamibayashi C (2015) Accepting foreign workers in Japanese society. University of Tokyo Press. [EL75-L64]

Kikuchi K, Tsutsumi M (2021) Inheritance of food culture among Okinawans in Brazil: the case of Sao Paulo. J Agric Dev Stud 31(3):29–37. [Z18-3132]

Massey DS, Arango J, Hugo G, Kouaouci A, Pellegrino A, Taylor JE (1993) Theories of international migration: a review and appraisal. Popul Dev Rev 19(3):431–466

Ministry of Education, Culture, Sports, Science and Technology (2001) A historical overview of 100 years of Japan's international student acceptance system. http://www.mext.go.jp/a_menu/koutou/ryugaku/011101/ayumi.pdf. Accessed 15 Apr 2025

Ministry of Education, Culture, Sports, Science and Technology, Ministry of Foreign Affairs, Ministry of Justice, Ministry of Health, Labour and Welfare, Ministry of Economy, Trade and Industry, Ministry of Land, Infrastructure, Transport and Tourism (2008) Outline of the '300,000 international student project'. https://www.mext.go.jp/a_menu/koutou/ryugaku/__icsFiles/afieldfile/2019/09/18/1420758_001.pdf. Accessed 25 Mar 2025

Ministry of Foreign Affairs (1878) Regulations for overseas passports (Notification No. 1). http://www.digital.archives.go.jp/das/image/F0000000000000013708. Accessed 15 May 2025

Ministry of Health, Labour and Welfare (2025) Summary of notification status of "Foreign employment situation" as of the end of June, 2024. https://www.mhlw.go.jp/content/11655000/001389442.pdf. Accessed 15 Apr 2025

Ministry of Home Affairs (1918) Matters concerning the entry of foreign nationals into Japan

Ministry of Justice (2012) About the new residence management system, vol 39. Akarenga: Newsletter of the Ministry of Justice. https://www.moj.go.jp/KANBOU/KOHOSHI/no39/2.html#report03. Accessed 15 Apr 2025

Ninomiya M (2014) Nikkei Brazil imin no rekishi to genzai (The history and present of Japanese–Brazilian immigrants). In: Bessatsu "Kan" 20: why the immigration issue now? Fujiwara Shoten. [DC812-L68], pp 341–347

Prime Minister's Office (2008) Policy speech by Prime Minister Fukuda at the 169th ordinary session of the Diet. http://www.kantei.go.jp/jp/hukudaspeech/2008/01/18housin.html. Accessed 15 May 2018
Sakugawa M, Aniya Y, Ohwan A, Yamaguchi H, Taba Y, Okawa M, Shimoji Y (2019) Culture of Okinawa prided and treasured by older first-generation Japanese–Bolivians from Okinawa. J Cult Nurs Stud 11(1):32–40. [Z74-G397]
Sassen S (2001) The global city: New York, London, Tokyo. Princeton University Press
Sommer BW (2006) Oral history and public memories. Temple University Press
Soysal YN (2021) Archives of displacement: migration, memory, and the politics of exile. Duke University Press
Takeda I (1991) The politics of immigration, refugees and aid. Keiso Shobo. [DC821-E19]
Takeda S (2006) Transition of the roles of Japan's international education policy: from foreign aid to global citizenship. Bull Graduate School Soc Cult Stud Nihon Univ J 7:79–90. [Z71-F183]
United Nations (n.d.) Definitions. https://refugeesmigrants.un.org/definitions. Accessed 25 Mar 2025
Vertovec S, Cohen R (2003) The age of migration: international population movements in the modern world. Palgrave Macmillan
Yoh K (2014) The history and current status of international student policy. Ann Bull Fac Hum Sci Matsuyama Shinonome Coll 22:51–75. [Z22-1726]
Yokota M, Shiratsuchi S (2004) International student advising. Nakanishiya Shuppan. [FD43-H60]
Zolberg AR (1981) International migration in political perspective. In: Kritz MM, Keely CB, Tomasi SM (eds) Global trends in migration: theory and research on international movements. Center for Migration Studies, pp 3–27
Zolberg AR (1989) Patterns of international migration policy. In: Appleyard R (ed) The impact of international migration on developing countries, pp 269–291

# Chapter 6
# How Has the Japanese Style of Organization Influenced Records Management and Information Disclosure Practices?

**Kazuhito Isomura**

**Abstract** This chapter aims to clarify how the Japanese style of organization has influenced records management and information disclosure practices. To clarify the nature of the Japanese style of organization, the chapter first reviews literature from the viewpoints of the duality of formal and informal organizations, the comparison of society and seken, and the characteristics of bureaucratic and administrative organizations. It then proposes hypotheses to serve as an analytical framework. Next, it examines three cases to understand how records management and information disclosure practices are affected by Japanese administrative organizations. Finally, it summarizes the main points of the chapter and proposes conclusions. In conclusion, while Japanese administrative organizations generally establish their records management systems effectively to preserve public records and personal notes, information disclosure often fails due to a tendency to avoid transparency in order to maintain insiders' human relationships and protect their interests.

**Keywords** Formal and informal organization · Society and seken · Bureaucratic and administrative organization · Records management · Information disclosure

## 6.1 Introduction

This chapter aims to clarify how the Japanese style of organization has influenced records management and information disclosure practices. It is often said that records management in Japan has not fully developed compared to that in Western countries. However, public records are systematically collected and preserved, particularly in Japanese administrative organizations. Public records are primarily created as a result of organizational activities. The methods of creating, accumulating,

---

K. Isomura (✉)
Faculty of Science and Engineering, Chuo University, Tokyo, Japan
e-mail: kisomura@tamacc.chuo-u.ac.jp



K. Fujiyoshi (ed.), *Governance, Ignorance, and Archives*,
https://doi.org/10.1007/978-981-95-1962-0_6

and utilizing records depends upon the nature of the organization that manages them. In fact, Shindo (2019) suggests that the characteristics of bureaucratic organizations in Japan are closely related to their approach to public records and information disclosure. Therefore, to understand the background of records management and information disclosure practices in Japan, this chapter theoretically examines how Japanese organizations are formed and function.

There are two major theories on records management: life cycle theory and record continuum theory. Life cycle theory focuses on the records themselves (Sletten 1999). It identifies the processes by which records are created, collected, accumulated, and selected for retention or destruction. Life cycle theory has been widely accepted by practitioners such as archivists and records managers because it explains how they manage archives and records in their workplaces. However, life cycle theory primarily emphasizes record retention rather than utilization. Consequently, a theoretical framework how to use record is needed.

In contrast, record continuum theory examines the relationship between individuals, organizations, and societies as key agents in creating various types of records through their activities (Piggott and McKemmish 2002; Upward 1996, 1997, 2001). Record continuum theory provides a framework for considering how these agents not only collect and accumulate records but also utilize them in their activities. Thus, record continuum theory is regarded as a foundational social theory of records. This chapter is based on record continuum theory to clarify how Japanese organizations create, collect, accumulate, select, destroy, and utilize records.

## 6.2 Research Method and Design

To clarify the Japanese style of organization, I review literature concerning basic organizational theories.

First, I consider the duality of formal and informal organizations. This duality is prevalent not only in Japanese organizations but also in organizations worldwide. However, the balance between formal and informal organizations varies by country, resulting in distinct cultural differences.

Second, to clarify these cultural differences, I examine the concept of "seken," in which Japanese organizations are embedded. Generally, seken is translated as society in English. However, the concept of seken differs significantly from that of society. I argue how seken functions in Japan compared to the concept of society in western countries.

Next, I explore the phenomena that seken creates within Japanese organizations. For example, phenomena such as "sontaku" or "kuki" occur. Seken is fundamentally created and operates among people who interact face-to-face in their workplaces. To maintain human relationships, individuals strive to understand the feelings or wishes of others. This attitude is referred to as sontaku, or "kuki wo yomu" (literally, reading the air), a phrase commonly used in Japan. Seken produces a strong collective effect known as sontaku or kuki, compelling individuals within a seken to conform to the expectations of others.

Third, I review literature on the functioning of bureaucratic organizations in Japan. Generally speaking, bureaucratic organizations are rational and impersonal, grounded in formal rules and procedures. However, when seken operates within bureaucratic organizations, Japanese bureaucratic organizations exhibit unique characteristics that differ from those in other countries. I specifically examine how Japanese administrative organizations differ from their counterparts in other nations.

Based on the literature reviews, I propose several working hypotheses to serve as an analytical framework to examine cases.

Next, I analyze cases using this analytical framework. I select three cases involving fraud within Japanese administrative organizations concerning records management and information disclosure. I investigate why issues such as non-disclosure of information, falsification, and cover-ups occur in these organizations.

Finally, I summarize the main points of this chapter and propose conclusions.

## 6.3 Literature Review

### *6.3.1 Formal and Informal Organizations*

Chester Barnard, the founder of organization theory, proposed two major concepts of organization: formal and informal organization (Barnard 1938; Isomura 2020, 2021, 2023). A formal organization is defined as "a system of consciously coordinated activities and forces of two or more persons" (Barnard 1938, p. 73). The formal organization comprises individuals' activities coordinated by a common organizational purpose. Therefore, formal organizations are fundamentally impersonal.

In contrast, an informal organization is defined as "the aggregate of the personal contacts and interactions and the associated groupings of people" (Barnard 1938, p. 115). The informal organization encompasses interactions between individuals and between individuals and groups. It consists of physical contacts, acts of cooperation, and verbal and nonverbal communication (Barnard 1948). Thus, the aggregate of human interactions is generally considered unintentional, intangible, and imponderable.

Barnard recognized the duality of formal and informal organizations, asserting that these organizations are inseparable. A formal organization comprises contributions from individuals; however, individuals also interact with one another through informal organizations. While the formal organization is depersonalized, the informal organization fosters individual personality and secures personal integrity.

Unlike formal organizations, informal organizations lack a common purpose. Consequently, formal organizations have a structure with subdivisions and special

**Table 6.1** The differences between formal and informal organizations

| Formal organization | Informal organization |
|---|---|
| Conscious organization coordinated by a common purpose | Unconscious organization without a common purpose |
| An impersonal system composed of contributors' activities | An aggregate of human interactions |
| A structural entity having some subdivisions and special organs to maintain itself | A structureless entity with no subdivisions |

*Source*: Isomura (2020)

organs such as executives and executive organizations, to maintain themselves; in contrast, informal organizations lack such structure.

Nevertheless, informal organizations yield common results from human interactions among individuals. For example, informal organizations establish certain attitudes, understandings, customs, habits, and institutions. They are generally considered the source of organizational culture and create informal networks and core groups when they function continuously in a cooperative system (Cross and Prusak 2002; Kleiner 2003; Krackhardt and Hanson 1993).

Overall, the common results produced by informal organizations significantly influence individuals' behaviors and ways of thinking, even though these results are often unconscious and unintentional. The differences between formal and informal organizations are summarized in Table 6.1.

Formal and informal organizations are closely interdependent and interrelated. First, informal organizations create the conditions under which formal organizations arise. Second, informal organizations cannot survive without formal organizations, as formal organizations provide the sustainable structure for society. An informal organization lacks a common purpose and does not establish stable relationships among individuals; therefore, it is inherently short-lived. To sustain itself, the informal organization relies on formal organizations, which stabilize social integration and structure society. Third, formal organizations serve as the basis for creating informal organizations. As formal organizations endure over time, they continuously generate human interactions among their contributors, who provide contributions to formal organizations, thereby inevitably fostering informal organizations.

Thus, formal and informal organizations are interdependent, each serving as the basis for the other's existence. They are interrelated, facilitating mutual survival and vitality.

The duality of formal and informal organizations is prevalent across cultures. However, the balance between formal and informal organizations varies by culture. In fact, cultural differences arise from which organization is dominant and how influential each organization is.

Consequently, the question of how to balance formal and informal organizations can be used to identify the culture an organization adopts. For example, Goffee and Jones (1996) categorize four different cultures based on two types of human

**Table 6.2** Organizational culture created by formal and informal organizations

| | Solidarity: Low | Solidarity: High |
|---|---|---|
| Sociability: High | Networked Culture | Communal Culture |
| Sociability: Low | Fragmented Culture | Mercenary Culture |

*Source*: Goffee and Jones (1996)

relations: sociability and solidarity. Sociability measures the degree of sincere friendliness among community members, while solidarity assesses a community's ability to effectively pursue shared objectives. Sociability and solidarity are closely related to informal and formal organizations, respectively. Goffee and Jones (1996) attempt to identify the organizational culture by examining how human relations are formed within an organization.

As Table 6.2 illustrates, based on these two measures, four cultures can be identified: a communal culture exhibits high sociability and solidarity; a mercenary culture has high solidarity but low sociability; a networked culture features high sociability but low solidarity; and a fragmented culture demonstrates low sociability and solidarity. Generally, it can be said that Japanese organizations adopt a networked culture, where informal organizations are more dominant than formal organizations, while Western organizations tend to create a mercenary culture, where formal organizations are more influential than informal organizations.

Thus, the question of how to balance formal and informal organizations is closely related to designing an effective organization that adapts to its environment.

In general, it can be said that formal organizations dominate in Western contexts, while informal organizations prevail in Japanese contexts. When formal organizations are more dominant than informal organizations, job descriptions, authority, and responsibility are clearly defined. In contrast, when informal organizations are more dominant than formal organizations, job descriptions, authority, and responsibility become vague and depend on individual decisions, thereby increasing individual discretion.

### *6.3.2 Society and Seken*

To understand how the Japanese style of organization functions in the workplace, the concept of "seken" is particularly useful. Seken clarifies how informal organizations are more dominant in Japan than formal organizations. The concept of seken differs significantly from that of society (Kato 2018). Abe is a leading researcher exploring the nature of seken, defining it as "personal human relationships, that is, a network of different people connected" or "a bond with their world where people are connected with their interests" (Abe 2003, p. 20). The understanding of the individual differs between Western and Japanese societies (Kato 2018). In Western societies, individuals are viewed as completely independent and create their society through relationships with others. In contrast, individuals in Japan are embedded in human relationships and are not necessarily regarded as independent. Therefore, the nature of personal human relationships in Japan is significantly different from that in Western countries (Abe 1995, 2003, 2006; Sato 2001, Kato 2018).

A seken serves as a reference group, and people are included as a member of seken when they are fully accepted. There are certain rules to be a member of seken: first, respect for elders; second, the importance of gift-giving and reciprocity, third, a sense of belonging to a shared temporal consciousness (Abe 2006).

A seken is inherently exclusive and discriminatory, making a sharp distinction between members and non-members. Consequently, individuals are strongly bound by a seken and are often not permitted to express personal opinions. Individuals do not bear personal responsibility for actions but they share their responsibility collectively (Abe 1995; Sato 2001).

Numerous informal rules govern behavior, and non-conformity can result in exclusion from a seken. Individuals exist within a closed organizational time-space. People in a seken have to share everything with others, and they must live in the same time and space (Abe 2006). A seken is not a traditional community united by blood ties or local connections; rather, it forms as quasi-community in a modern society.

A seken fosters a strong conformity known as "kuki" (Yamamoto 1977; Kogami 2009, 2019). Kuki, literally meaning air, refers to the organizational atmosphere that people have to follow. People are constantly required to understand kuki, which creates pressure to conform, compelling individuals to guess the thoughts and feelings of others. They do not want to say or behave against other people's expectations. This phenomenon is termed "sontaku" (Enomoto 2017).

Sontaku is a common behavior that people often adopt in seken. For instance, when a superior does not provide direct formal instructions, subordinates often sense and understand their superior's desires through informal communication. Consequently, subordinates are expected to be attuned to the organizational atmosphere known as kuki (Enomoto 2017). Mito (2018) noted that sontaku is particularly prevalent when informal organizations dominate over formal organizations.

Kuki can create a stifling atmosphere, inhibiting individuals from freely expressing their thoughts. Members are generally discouraged from voicing opposition; kuki exerts influence that encourages unanimous adherence to the rules of seken (Kogami 2009, 2019). Thus, reading kuki involves sensing others' intentions and discerning their desires. As a result, many individuals may refrain from expressing their own thoughts directly.

Even if someone perceives a situation as problematic but does not want to conform, they may be unable to voice their concerns due to their membership in a seken. Consequently, they cannot distrust fellow members and must leave their questions unaddressed.

In a seken prevalent in Japan, superiors do not necessarily exert coercive power, as subordinates instinctively strive to understand and follow their superiors' feelings and intentions. Those who successfully interpret their superiors' intentions can promote rapidly. According to Enomoto (2017), many individuals in Japan tend to act in ways that do not disappoint others' expectations. They avoid conflict and engage in communication to build and maintain rapport.

However, it is important to note that organizational mechanisms also create strong conformity in Western-style organizations. For example, the functions of sontaku and kuki are similar to the concept of group think proposed by Janis (Janis 1972). Janis (1972) examined the effect of group dynamics that create strong pressures for conformity, preventing members from expressing dissent. Additionally, Kleiner (2003, 2005) argues that in Western cultures, individuals form core groups within organizations, compelling others to follow the core group's intentions. Thus, it can be concluded that sontaku and kuki serve as mechanisms in Japanese organizations that foster strong conformity.

### 6.3.3 Bureaucratic and Administrative Organizations

This section examines the nature of bureaucratic and administrative organizations in Japan. First, I will review the theoretical underpinnings of bureaucratic organizations. Then, I will analyze how administrative organizations function in practice in Japan.

Generally, Michels and Weber are considered pioneers in emphasizing the importance of bureaucratic organizations (Michels 1915; Weber 1947). Michels posits that as organizations develop, stratification occurs, leading to a small number of leaders dominating the majority of members. He refers to this as the iron law of oligarchy. Conversely, Weber characterizes bureaucratic organizations as pyramid-shaped entities with a hierarchical structure, featuring one leader at the top and multiple strata below.

Nishio (2001) summarizes that modern bureaucratic organizations, as defined by Weber, constitute the following principles: (1) discipline through formal rules, (2) rigid division of authority, (3) formal lines of authority, (4) distinction between private and public property, (5) elimination of hereditary privileges, (6) all decisions and rules recorded in writing, (7) an appointive system, (8) a contract system, (9) qualifications evaluated based on educational history and expertise, (10) fixed salaries paid in monetary form, (11) full-time officials, and (12) career advancement based on job tenure and performance.

According to Nishio (2001), principles (1) through (6) primarily relate to the organization of bureaucratic entities, enhancing predictability and depersonalization. In contrast, principles (7) through (12) pertain to personnel systems, establishing the foundational principles for government officials.

Weber emphasizes the rationality of bureaucracy, generally highlighting its positive aspects, while Bendix, Blau, and Merton focus on its negative aspects (Merton 1940, 1949; Blau 1955, Bendix 1956). Merton, in particular, examines the dysfunctions of bureaucracy, emphasizing the irrational behaviors that can arise within bureaucratic organizations. While bureaucracy is typically viewed as rational and functional, informal organizations can obstruct formal organizations from functioning effectively.

From the clients' perspective, bureaucracy offers predictability and depersonalization. However, when assessing a bureaucracy's effectiveness in achieving its organizational goals, its performance is related to organizational effectiveness and efficiency. Therefore, even though an organization adopts the principles of bureaucracy, how different types of bureaucratic organization achieve their performance depends upon its objectives (Nishio 2001).

For instance, in a military organization, the principle of unity of command is strictly adhered to. The military organization centralizes decision-making and operates as a closed system, entirely separated from the external environment. In contrast, an administrative organization is a complex entity composed of multiple unit organizations that operate in parallel, each with its own objectives. This results in a complicated network of communication channels throughout the organization. Consequently, decision-making is typically decentralized. In addition, an administrative organization is involved not only in policy implementation but also in policy-making alongside politicians. Thus, administrative organizations are complex and may not strictly adhere to bureaucratic principles.

I will now examine the nature of Japanese administrative organizations in comparison to those of Western countries (Nishio 2001; Omori 2006, Shindo 2019). Generally, an administrative organization is divided into unit organizations such as ministries, bureaus, divisions, sections, and units. Each affair under jurisdiction is typically allocated to a specific unit organization level. In Western administrative organizations, matters are usually divided at the section level, while in Japan, they are divided at the division level. The assignments within a section are not rigidly determined and can be adjusted based on circumstances (Nishio 2001).

Additionally, in Western countries, each member and their secretary typically have individual offices; in contrast, in Japan, individuals generally work together in relatively large rooms, with personal offices often reserved for higher ranking officials (Omori 2006). Furthermore, administrative organizations are intricate, divided both vertically and horizontally. Consequently, completely different matters may be assigned to a single unit organization.

When an organization is divided horizontally, subordinate organizations may not be necessarily subjected to their superior organizations but instead fall under the strong control of various secretariat organizations as a cabinet bureau of personnel affairs is established (Nishio 2001). In Japanese administrative organizations, the national government organization law primarily defines the structure of labor division but does not prescribe how matters under jurisdiction are vertically divided.

The job ranking system typically clarifies roles and responsibility in each ranking; however, in Japan, administrative organizations often lack such clarity. As a result, decision-making processes within Japanese administrative organizations can be ambiguous. According to Nishio (2001), there are three distinct types of decision-making: top-down, bottom-up, and combinations of the two. For example, three ranks—Director General, Director, and Deputy Director—may share responsibilities and utilize different decision-making approaches in their roles. Top-down decision-making involves direct instructions, while bottom-up decision-making involves approvals; combinations utilize both methods.

Moreover, administrative organizations are obligated to follow dual responsibilities: following the law and obeying their superiors' instructions. Superior instructions are categorized into two steps: first, they must comply with administrative rules; second, they are made in the context of specific roles.

Administrative rules are documented, which can lead to confusion with administrative laws. However, they are distinct from laws. It is impossible to define every aspect by law; thus, discretion remains. Conflicts often arise between discipline and discretion. In practice, those responsible for their roles can exercise judgment when making decisions.

As Bendix (1956) points out, the central challenge for bureaucratic organizations is balancing the conflict between discipline and discretion, as well as between obedience and autonomy. Therefore, it is essential to recognize that bureaucratic and administrative organizations do not necessarily apply to an organization that works only on fixed rules and procedures.

### *6.3.4 Analytical Framework of this Chapter*

On the basis of those literature reviews, I propose three hypotheses. These hypotheses will be used to analyze the three cases presented in the following section.

Hypothesis 1: In Japanese organizations, informal organizations are more dominant than formal organizations. Consequently, individuals tend to underestimate the importance of adhering to formal rules in order to maintain human relationships.

Hypothesis 2: In Japanese organizations, the function of seken operates strongly, leading to separation from the external world. When problems arise, they are often concealed to protect personal interests.

Hypothesis 3: In Japanese administrative organizations, job roles, authority, and responsibilities are loosely defined, allowing government officials to act arbitrarily by exercising their discretion.

In the next section, I will examine three cases where records management and information disclosure practices are significantly influenced by the Japanese style of organization.

## 6.4 Case Study

Several political scandals related to public records management and information disclosure have emerged since the 2000s, including the Moritomo Gakuen scandal, the Kake Gakuen scandal, the Defense Minister daily reports scandal, and the Cherry Blossom Viewing Party scandal.

I will analyze three cases to illustrate how the Japanese style of organization, particularly within Japanese administrative organizations, has strongly influenced public records management and information disclosure practices.

### 6.4.1 The Moritomo Gakuen Scandal

The Moritomo Gakuen scandal arose when Moritomo Gakuen purchased government-owned land at a significantly discounted price. Prime Minister Abe's wife served as the honorary principal of the institution. Allegations surfaced that Prime Minister Abe or his wife were involved in the unfair discounting of government-owned land.

The main issue revolves around the existence of public records that clarify the process by which this discount was implemented and the involvement of Prime Minister Abe or his wife. Table 6.3 summarizes the overview of this scandal.

According to Akagi's personal notes, Sagawa, Director-General of the Financial Bureau, instructed Sugita, Kinki Finance Bureau, to falsify public records (Akagi and Aizawa 2020). Sugita then ordered Akagi to falsify public records through Ikeda, Akagi's direct superior. Akagi was directed to falsify every part of public records to benefit Moritomo Gakuen and to provide the related records to the Board of Audit as minimally as possible.

Reports on the falsification of officially approved records clarify that records were not destroyed but preserved. They identify the parts where the Ministry of Finance instructed the falsification of public records (Ministry of Finance 2018). The reports also clarify that public officials at the Kinki Finance Bureau strongly resisted the falsification of public records. Sagawa, Director-General of the Financial Bureau, stated in the Diet that all related records had been destroyed at the discretion of the Ministry of Finance. However, it is common practice for such records to be preserved permanently as office materials.

Overall, in this case, public records were systematically falsified under the orders of the Ministry of Finance. The Ministry attempted to avoid information disclosure by claiming that the records related to the issue had already been destroyed. However, the records had been preserved. The truth was not revealed until an insider disclosed the systematic falsification. Although the falsification was not ordered by the Prime Minister, it was initiated by the Ministry of Finance to protect the Prime Minister and his wife voluntarily. It remains unclear whether the Director-General of the Financial Bureau directly instructed the falsification of public records; however, the Deputy-General was later promoted to Commissioner of National Taxes.

### 6.4.2 The Kake Gakuen Scandal

The establishment of a new school of veterinary medicine had not been approved for over 50 years, both by the regulations of the Ministry of Education, Culture, Sports, Science, and Technology (MEXT) and by pressure from the Japan Veterinary Medicine Association. However, the National Strategic Special Zones (NSSZ), which promote regulatory relaxation, proposed the establishment of a school of veterinary medicine. Subsequently, Kake Gakuen, managed by Kake Kotaro, who is closely associated with Prime Minister Abe, received approval to establish a school of veterinary medicine.

**Table 6.3** Overview of the Moritomo Gakuen Scandal

| Date | Event |
|---|---|
| February 8, 2017 | The City Council of Toyonaka City filed a lawsuit requesting information disclosure, revealing that Moritomo Gakuen had purchased government-owned land at a significantly discounted price. |
| February 9, 2017 | Asahi Shimbun published an article stating that the land, valued at 0.9 billion yen, had been discounted by over 0.8 billion yen. |
| February 17, 2017 | Prime Minister Abe was questioned in the Diet regarding the issue. He stated that he would resign as Prime Minister and Diet member if he or his wife were involved in the discount. |
| February 24, 2017 | Sagawa, Director-General of the Financial Bureau, responded to questions in the Diet, claiming that no public records existed related to the negotiation process and that any relevant records had been already destroyed. |
| February 26, 2017 | The falsification of public records began. |
| March 7, 2017 | The Board of Audit decided to initiate a special examination to determine whether the sale of government-owned land was appropriate or involved unfair discounting. |
| April 11 to 13, 2017 | The Ministry of Finance explained that they had not preserved any records related to the negotiation of the sale. |
| June 23, 2017 | The Kinki Finance Bureau transferred all staff members involved in the sale to different workplaces, and records related to the sale were destroyed. |
| June 28, 2017 | The Special Investigation Squad of the Osaka District Public Prosecutors Office requested the Kinki Finance Bureau to provide the records voluntarily. |
| July 15, 2017 | Akagi, who was ordered to falsify public records, was diagnosed with depression. |
| July 20, 2017 | Akagi took a sick leave and later received a leave of absence. |
| November 17, 2017 | Akagi was requested for optional questioning by the Special Investigation Squad of the Osaka District Public Prosecutors Office. |
| December 25, 2017 | Akagi received a phone call from a prosecutor. |
| February 22, 2018 | Akagi documented his records of disease as personal notes. |
| March 2, 2018 | The falsification of public records became public. |
| March 7, 2018 | Akagi, who had been pressured to falsify public records by his superior, committed suicide. |
| March 9, 2018 | Sagawa resigned as Commissioner of National Taxes. |
| March 12, 2018 | The Minister of Finance admitted that the falsification of public records had occurred. |
| June 4, 2018 | Ministry of Finance released reports on the falsification of officially approved records. |

*Source*: Asahi Shimbun news crews (2018)

Allegations arose that Prime Minister Abe was involved in this approval. A critical issue in this scandal was whether public records existed to clarify the roles of the Special Advisor to the Prime Minister, the Deputy Director-General of the Minister's Secretariat, and the Deputy Chief Cabinet Secretary in lobbying MEXT for approval by favoring the Prime Minister's intentions. Table 6.4 summarizes the overview of this scandal.

**Table 6.4** Overview of the Kake Gakuen Scandal

| Date | Event |
|---|---|
| April 2, 2015 | Section chiefs from Ehime Prefecture and Imabari City, along with the bureau chief of Kake Gakuen, visited the official residence of the Prime Minister and met with a Special Advisor to the Prime Minister. |
| June 2015 | Ehime Prefecture and Imabari City proposed establishing a new school of veterinary medicine in a NSSZ. The Abe government made a cabinet decision outlining four conditions for approving a new school of veterinary medicine. |
| January 29, 2016 | Imabari City was designated as a NSSZ. |
| March 2016 | Kyoto Prefecture and Kyoto Sangyo University proposed establishing a new school of veterinary medicine in a NSSZ. |
| September to October 2016 | Special Advisor to the Prime Minister met with the Vice-Minister of MEXT at the Prime Minister's official residence. Records were created that included phrases such as "Prime Minister's intentions" and "those who are at the top level in the official residence of the Prime Minister suggested that." |
| November 9, 2016 | For the first time in fifty-two years, the establishment of a new school of veterinary medicine was approved. However, an additional condition was imposed: it could only set up "in a broad area where there are no existing schools of veterinary medicine." |
| January 12, 2017 | The Advisory Committee of NSSZ officially approved the plan for Kake Gakuen to establish a school of veterinary medicine in Imabari City. |
| March 28, 2017 | Prime Minister Abe was questioned in the Diet about his involvement in the approval of Kake Gakuen's establishment of a school of veterinary medicine. He responded, "If I were involved in the decision, I would take responsibility". |
| May 17, 2017 | Asahi Shimbun reported that public records existed in MEXT that included phrases such as "Prime Minister's intentions" and "those who are at the top level in the official residence of the Prime Minister suggested that." |
| May 19, 2017 | MEXT reported the results of its investigation at a press conference, stating that the Ministry was not able to find such public records. |
| May 23, 2017 | Maekawa, the former Vice-Minister of MEXT, admitted the fact that the public records reported by Asahi Shimbun did exist. |
| May 25, 2017 | Maekawa held a press conference, stating that he was not able to hide the truth. |
| June 9, 2017 | MEXT announced that it would make an additional investigation into the public records. |
| June 15, 2017 | MEXT apologized and acknowledged that they were able to identify fourteen public records out of nineteen that included phrases such as "Prime Minister's intentions." |
| August 25, 2017 | The Council for University Chartering and School Juridical Person suspended its decision to approve Kake Gakuen's establishment of a new school of veterinary medicine. |

(continued)

**Table 6.4** (continued)

| Date | Event |
|---|---|
| November 10, 2017 | MEXT announced that the Council for University Chartering and School Juridical Person had submitted a report that they had approved Kake Gakuen's establishment of a new school of veterinary medicine. |
| November 14, 2017 | MEXT officially approved Kake Gakuen's establishment of the new school of veterinary medicine. |
| April 3, 2018 | Kake Gakuen held the entrance ceremony for the school of veterinary medicine at Okayama University of Science. |
| April 10, 2018 | Asahi Shimbun reported that public records related to the April 2, 2015 meeting created by Ehime Prefecture existed. According to these records, the Special Advisor to the Prime Minister stated that setting up a new school of veterinary medicine was a "Prime Minister matter." |
| April 10, 2018 | In the morning, the Special Advisor to the Prime Minister claimed that he had not meet anyone from Ehime Prefecture or Imabari City. |
| April 10, 2018 | The Governor of Ehime Prefecture confirmed that the records were created as a memorandum to inform prefectural staff members about the meeting's discussions. |
| April 13, 2018 | Ministry of Agriculture, Forestry and Fisheries clarified that it had found public records within the ministry that contained similar content. |
| April 20, 2018 | MEXT clarified that it had discovered emails from the Cabinet Office indicating that the Special Advisor to the Prime Minister had an appointment to meet with Ehime Prefectural staff members. |
| May 10, 2018 | Special Advisor to the Prime Minister admitted at the House of Representatives Budget Committee that he had met with staff members from Kake Gakuen three times. |

*Source*: Asahi Shimbun news crews (2018)

Overall, in this case, numerous related public records were preserved in each organization. However, the handling of these records was ambiguous, leading some to be classified as personal notes or memoranda. Consequently, it was not necessarily clear whether these records are official or not. The existence of these records was revealed because the Prime Minister was questioned in the Diet about his involvement and because newspapers made a report on this issue. In general, those records are not disclosed. Without whistleblowers to leak pertinent information, the facts and records remain concealed from the public.

### *6.4.3 The Self-Defense Forces' Daily Reports Scandal*

This scandal emerged when a journalist requested the Ministry of Defense to disclose the Self-Defense Forces' Daily Reports. Initially, the ministry responded that the information could not be disclosed because it had already been destroyed. Subsequently, a newspaper then pointed out that destroying important public records is a serious problem for records management.

Ministry of Defense started to investigate whether or not daily reports had indeed been destroyed. It was then revealed that the reports had been preserved within the

**Table 6.5** Overview of the Self-Defense Forces' Daily Reports Scandal

| Date | Event |
|---|---|
| September 30, 2016 | A journalist requested the Ministry of Defense to disclose the Self-Defense Forces' Daily Reports. |
| November 20, 2016 | Self-Defense Forces sent an advance party of 130 members to South Sudan, assigned a new mission to "rush to rescue" and "protect and guide encampment." |
| November 22, 2016 | In the Diet, opposing parties pointed out that the PKO (peacekeeping operation) in South Sudan was in a serious security condition and that what had been recorded as "sento (battle)" in March had been rewritten as "shototsu (collision)." |
| December 2, 2016 | Ministry of Defense informed the journalist that the daily reports had already been destroyed and therefore could not be disclosed. |
| December 14, 2016 | Kanagawa Shimbun reported that the daily reports had been destroyed. |
| December 24, 2016 | Chunichi Shimbun reported similar news. |
| February 6, 2017 | Kono announced via X (formerly, Twitter) that the daily reports had been found in the ministry. |
| February 9, 2017 | Ministry of Defense retracted its previous decision not to disclose the daily reports, opting to disclose the reports from six days, July 7 to July 12. The reports from July 11 and 12 were fully disclosed, while the other four reports were partially disclosed by being blacked out. |
| February 13, 2017 | The daily reports were disclosed to the journalist. |

*Source*: Fuse and Miura (2020)

ministry and were eventually disclosed. The Ministry of Defense had systematically attempted to hide the existence of these daily reports and avoid making this information public.

Overview of this scandal is summarized in Table 6.5. The systematic concealment of daily reports by the Ministry of Defense is summarized in Table 6.6.

This scandal reveals that the Ministry of Defense has a habit of concealing inconvenient truths. In fact, when such truths were exposed, the Ministry attempted to hide them systematically. Furthermore, the Ministry avoided disclosing information in response to journalists' requests, citing that records were designated for destruction within a year and had already been destroyed. However, most records had been preserved. The daily reports were retained and used by various sections in the Ministry. Even after the reports were discovered, the Ministry continued its systematic concealment efforts.

## 6.5 Discussion and Conclusion

This section summarizes the main points of the chapter and examines the cases through the hypotheses.

In the first case, public records were properly preserved. However, when issues arose and related records were requested for disclosure, the Kinki Finance Bureau did not respond, claiming the records had already been destroyed. The statements

**Table 6.6** The Process of Hiding the daily reports

| Date | Event |
|---|---|
| December 16, 2016 | Ministry of Defense instructed its staff to search for daily reports. |
| December 26, 2016 | The daily reports were located in the Joint Staff Office. |
| January 24, 2017 | Prime Minister Abe stated in the Diet that the daily reports did not exist in the Ministry of Defense. |
| January 27, 2017 | The fact that the daily reports were found was informed to Inada, the Minister of Defense. However, it took over a month for the Minister to know this fact after the reports were found. The Ministry of Defense then attempted to systematically hide this fact. The daily reports contained detailed accounts of battle situations spanning more than 50 pages. |
| March 10, 2017 | Self-Defense Forces decided to withdraw 350 troops from South Sudan by the end of May. |
| March 16, 2017 | The Inspector General's Office of Legal Compliance resolved to implement Special Defense Inspection. |
| July 19, 2017 | NHK reported on the scandal involving Inada, the Minister of Defense, who attempted to conceal the existence of the daily reports. In fact, the Ministry of Defense held an emergent meeting to discuss how to address the issue related to the daily reports. Attendees included the Minister, Vice-Minister, Minister's Secretariat, Chief of Staff of the Ground Self-Defense Force (G.S.D.F.), and the Vice Chief of Staff of the G.S.D.F. |
| July 27, 2017 | Minister, Vice-Minister, and Chief of Staff of the G.S.D.F. resigned. |
| July 28, 2018 | Investigation reports were published, revealing that the Ministry of Defense had systematically concealed the facts. |

*Source*: Fuse and Miura (2020)

made by the Prime Minister and the Director-General of the Financial Bureau in the Diet led to disclosure and falsify them. It is assumed that the Ministry of Finance and the Kinki Finance Bureau interpreted the Prime Minister's expectations and acted accordingly. Sontaku worked strongly and no evidence was found to clarify that the Prime Minister issued any instructions in this scandal. As Hypothesis 1 suggests, administrative organizations underestimated the importance of adhering to formal rules in favor of maintaining interpersonal relationships, leading to the falsification of approved public records.

In the second case, public records were similarly well-maintained. After opposition parties questioned the Prime Minister in the Diet regarding his involvement in favoring a close friend for the approval of a new veterinary medicine school, he denied the allegations. Subsequent newspaper articles reported that the Special Advisor to the Prime Minister pressured the Ministry of Education, Culture, Sports, Science, and Technology (MEXT) to approve the school on the Prime Minister's behalf. However, the Special Advisor denied having met with the Vice-Minister of MEXT at the official residence. This led to an examination of whether public records related to the scandal have been preserved. Initially, MEXT announced that no public records existed. However, after the former Vice-Minister of MEXT insisted that relevant records were available, they were subsequently found. Thus, while public records are generally created and preserved, only insiders are aware of their locations and contents. Outsiders cannot know what records are preserved unless issues arise and strong public opinion demands disclosure. Additionally, some records are regarded to be informal because they are personal notes rather than public records, and therefore are not considered necessary for disclosure. As Hypotheses 1 and 2 suggest, the relevant administrative organizations prioritized government interests and intentionally avoided disclosing public records.

In the third case, public records were preserved similarly to the first and second cases. However, when requests for information disclosure were made, those records were not disclosed, as if they had already been destroyed. In reality, while paper records are often officially destroyed, their electronic counterparts are secretly retained. Only insiders know where and what public records are still kept. Consequently, when disclosing information is inconvenient for the Ministry of Defense, the Ministry attempted to avoid disclosing related public records. Thus, the decision to disclose information depends on the Ministry's judgment. As Hypotheses 2 and 3 suggest, the administrative organization sought to protect its interests and abused its discretion.

In these three cases, it can be concluded that administrative organizations generally maintain their records systematically and properly. Indeed, precise records are preserved, including personal notes. However, they often avoid disclosure in response to information requests. Administrative organizations designate records for destruction within a year and claim that records requested for disclosure have already been destroyed. In practice, they destroy paper records while secretly preserving electronic files (Mainichi Shimbun news crews 2020).

It can be asserted that administrative organizations in Japan have effectively developed their records management systems and can locate their preserved records. However, they frequently employ tactics to avoid information disclosure by manipulating file names, making it difficult to identify what information is preserved (Mainichi Shimbun news crews 2020). Therefore, the issue is not due to an inefficient records management system, despite criticisms that Japan's records management systems are underdeveloped. The manner in which information is disclosed is more critical than the records management system itself.

In most cases, even if records are preserved, they are not necessarily disclosed. For instance, if records are preserved, they may be classified as personal notes rather than public records (Mainichi Shimbun news crews 2020). Consequently, these personal notes are considered exempt from disclosure. Administrative organizations exercise discretion and handle records arbitrarily. Even when records are preserved, cover-ups occur. When records are disclosed, they are often redacted. In some cases, systematic falsification is done.

The problem primarily pertains to information disclosure. There exists a huge information gap between insiders and outsiders. Outsiders are often unaware of what records are preserved within administrative organizations. Insiders, seeking to maintain their relationships and protect their interests, frequently claim that requested public records do not exist or refuse to disclose them.

In conclusion, the Japanese style of organization has profoundly influenced records management and information disclosure practices. To address this issue, it is essential to build a technologically advanced records management system that limits public administrators' discretion and arbitrariness. Additionally, it would be beneficial to create a database that accumulates all disclosed information in response to requests for information disclosure, ensuring public access (Kusakabe 2018). Administrative organizations should compile a list of created and preserved records and adhere to formal rules and guidelines to ensure that these records are disclosed to the public.

## References

Abe K (1995) Seken toha nanika (What a seken is) (in Japanese). Kodansha, Tokyo (KG748-E266)
Abe K (2003) Nihon shakai de ikiru koto (Living in Japanese society) (in Japanese). Asahi Shimbun, Tokyo (GB61-H4)
Abe K (2006) Kindaika to seken (Modernization and seken) (in Japanese). Asahi Shimbun, Tokyo (GB31-L10)
Akagi M, Aizawa F (2020) Watashi wa shinjutsu ga shiritai (I want to know the truth) (in Japanese). Bungeishunju, Tokyo (AZ-311-M85)
Asahi Shimbun news crews (2018) Kenryoku no haishin (Betrayal of power) (in Japanese). Asahi Shimbun Publishing, Tokyo (GB571-L434)
Barnard CI (1938) The functions of the executive. Harvard University Press, Cambridge, MA
Barnard CI (1948) Organization and management: selected papers. Harvard University Press, Cambridge, MA
Bendix R (1956) Work and authority in industry: ideologies of management in the course of industrialization. Wiley, New York
Blau PM (1955) The dynamics of bureaucracy: a study of interpersonal relations in two Government agencies. University of Chicago Press, Chicago, IL
Cross R, Prusak L (2002) The people who make organizations go-or stop. Harv Bus Rev:105–112
Enomoto H (2017) Sontaku no kozo (The structure of sontaku) (in Japanese). East Press, Tokyo (EC221-L330)
Fuse Y, Miura H (2020) Nippo inpei (Hiding daily reports) (in Japanese). Shueisha, Tokyo (A159-M9)
Goffee R, Jones G (1996) What holds the modern company together? Harv Bus Rev November–December:133–148
Isomura K (2020) Organization theory by Chester Barnard: an introduction. Springer, Singapore
Isomura K (2021) Management theory by Chester Barnard: an introduction. Springer, Singapore
Isomura K (2023) Chester I. Barnard: innovator of organization theory. Springer, Singapore
Janis IL (1972) Victims of groupthink: a psychological study of foreign-policy decisions and fiascoes. Houghton Mifflin, Boston
Kato H (2018) Shakaigaku: watashi to seken (Sociology: seken and I) (in Japanese). Chuokoron Shinsha, Tokyo (EC1-L253)
Kleiner A (2003) Are you in with the in crowd? Harv Bus Rev July:86–92
Kleiner A (2005) Who really matters: the core group theory of power, privilege, and success. Doubleday, New York
Kogami S (2009) Kuki to seken (Air and seken) (in Japanese). Kodansha, Tokyo (KH279-J234)
Kogami S (2019) Kuki wo yondemo shitagawanai (Do not follow kuki even if reading the air) (in Japanese). Iwanami Shoten, Tokyo (Y5-N19-M240)
Krackhardt D, Hanson JR (1993) Informal networks: the company behind the chart. Harv Bus Rev July–August:104–111

Kusakabe S (2018) Buki toshiteno joho kokai (Information disclosure as a weapon) (in Japanese). Chikuma Shobo Shinsha, Tokyo (AZ-311-L335)

Mainichi Shimbun news crews (2020) Kobunsho kiki (Crisis in public records) (in Japanese). Mainichi Shimbun Publishing, Tokyo (AZ-311-M79)

Merton R (1949) Social theory and social structure: toward the codification of theory and research. Free Press, New York

Michels R (1915) Political parties: a sociological study of the oligarchical tendencies of modern democracy. Jarrold, London

Ministry of Finance (2018) Kessai bunsho no kaizan tonikansuru chosa hokokusyo (Reports on falsification of officially approved records). https://www.mof.go.jp/public_relations/statement/other/20180604chousahoukoku.pdf. Accessed 11 Jan 2024

Mito T (2018) Sontaku no keiegaku (Management theory on sontaku). Paper presented at Kanto's area meeting of Japan Academy of Business Administration, Nihon University, May 26, 2018

Nishio M (2001) Gyoseigaku shinpan (Public administration new edition) (in Japanese). Yuhikaku, Tokyo (A311-G66)

Omori W (2006) Kan no shisutemu (The system of public administration) (in Japanese). University of Tokyo Press, Tokyo (AZ-331-H22)

Piggott M, McKemmish S (2002) Recordkeeping, reconciliation and political reality. Presented at Australian society of archivists annual conference, Sydney, Australia

Sato N (2001) Seken no genshogaku (Phenomelogy of seken) (in Japanese). Seikyusha, Toyko (EC71-G76)

Shindo M (2019) Kanryosei to kobunsho (Bureacracy and public records) (in Japanese). Chikuma Syobo Shinsha, Tokyo (AZ-311-M30)

Sletten L (1999) Lessons from down under: records management in Australia. Inf Manage J 33(1):26–32

Upward F (1996) Structuring the records continuum, part one: postcustodial principles and properties. Archiv Manuscripts 24(2):268–285

Upward F (1997) Structuring the records continuum, part two: structuration theory and recordkeeping. Archiv Manuscripts 25(1):10–35

Upward F (2001) Modelling the continuum as paradigm shift in recordkeeping and archiving processes, and beyond a personal reflection. Record Manage J 10(3):115–139

Weber M (1947) The theory of social and economic organization. Free Press, New York

Yamamoto S (1977) Kuki no Kenkyu (A study on reading the air) (in Japanese). Bungeishunju, Tokyo (EB98-412)

# Chapter 7
# Public Recordkeeping System and Professionals in Japan: Focusing on the "Standard of Tasks and Competencies for Archivist"

**Naoki Shimoju**

**Abstract** The development of Japan's public recordkeeping system and the archivist profession is discussed in this chapter, focusing on the Standard of Tasks and Competencies for Archivist (STCA) developed by the National Archives of Japan in 2018. Public Records and Archives management in Japan began in the mid-nineteenth century and developed while experiencing record loss due to war and disaster. After World War II, interest in archives management in politics and government was low, but demand by academic researchers was high, and the importance of archives management was reaffirmed in the 2000s. The year 2009 saw the enactment of the Public Records and Archives Management Act, and the National Archives of Japan developed the STCA to establish a professional system for archivist, and in 2020 a "certified archivist" system was initiated, and the profession is being established. However, issues of employment instability, compensation, and professional education remain, and there is a need to enhance education and careers for the digital age.

**Keywords** Standard of Tasks and Competencies for Archivist (STCA) · National Archives of Japan · Japan Society for Archival Science (JSAS) · Yasuo Fukuda · Certified Archivists · Associate Certified Archivists · Profession · Training and Education of Archivists

## 7.1 Introduction

In Japan, the public records and archive management system began in the mid-nineteenth century. This coincided with the formation of a modern centralized governance structure and bureaucracy modeled after Europe. To ensure that the new

N. Shimoju (✉)
Graduate School of Humanities, Gakushuin University, Tokyo, Japan
e-mail: naoki.shimoju@gakushuin.ac.jp



K. Fujiyoshi (ed.), *Governance, Ignorance, and Archives*,
https://doi.org/10.1007/978-981-95-1962-0_7

government, which replaced the Edo shogunate, was able to govern the country, the cabinet and ministries were required to maintain and accumulate records, along with a system for determining and communicating government decisions, such as laws and regulations, through official documents that were established at the beginning of the cabinet system in 1885. However, during the Great Kanto Earthquake of September 1923, many central ministries and agencies lost most of their records and the opportunity to create their own archives.

Fortunately, the Ministry of Foreign Affairs, which was not damaged by the fire caused by the earthquake, attempted to preserve the vast number of records and organize them into an archive for using in foreign policy decisions. The Ministry of Foreign Affairs sent senior officials to Europe, which had the most advanced education system at the time, to use the results of their studies at the Ecole des Chartres in France to manage their records and create a system of archives. However, this was an exception to the rule, and many central ministries experienced the loss of even more records during the subsequent air raids by the U.S. military during World War II and the confusion caused by the defeat in the war.

Amid postwar reconstruction and economic growth, the management of public records came to emphasize prompt decision-making and organizational efficiency. By the last half of the twentieth century, Japan's successful political, administrative, and business leaders had lost the idea of reviewing. However, the demand for the preservation and publication of records and archives to review the past flourished in the academic community, particularly among historians, as exemplified by Ezra Feivel Vogel's (1930–2020) bestseller *Japan as Number One: Lessons for America* published in 1979, which also supported the growing popularity for "Japanese studies" outside of Japan and the insistence of Japanese scholars that the government establish a system of archives.

How does the Japanese archivist, born into a contradictory social structure of low interest in the political and administrative spheres and high interest among academic scholars, have an institutional base, and what is it attempting to achieve?

This study focuses on the document "Standard of Tasks and Competencies for Archivist (STCA)," established by the National Archives of Japan in December 2018, and introduces the challenges in terms of training and education for archivists.

## 7.2 Development of the "Standard of Tasks and Competencies for Archivist": Background and Objectives

The Public Archives Act, enacted in 1987, regulates the existence of archivists and their role in archival institutions in Japan. This act was implemented against the backdrop of the energetic activities of scholars and archivists studying Archival Science in Europe and North America during the 1980s. The Records and Archives Management Programme (RAMP) documents, on which UNESCO was working in cooperation with the International Council on Archives (ICA), played a significant role in the intellectual background that enabled these activities to continue. In particular, in relation to ICA, the recommendations made by Michael Roper (1932–2024), who visited Japan as its emissary, provided further intellectual stimulation.

Furthermore, political power was required to establish this basic act on archives. Niro Iwakami (1913–1989), who served as the governor of Ibaraki Prefecture and then the director of the Ibaraki Prefectural Museum of History, became a member of the House of Councilors in 1977 and patiently lobbied the Diet for a law that would address the needs of the community involved in archives.

However, this Act was intended only for the archives of national and local governments, and the role of archivists was extremely rudimentary and limited to research and study for selecting public records based on their historical value. Furthermore, there was a special exception, in that local archives did not have to employ professionals, and this has not changed to this day.

This reflects the fact that a system for educating archivists has not yet been established in Japanese society. The absence of leadership in the archival community has also allowed inaction by the government and local governments to solve such problems.

This situation began to change during the 2000s, with the establishment of the Japan Society for Archival Science (JSAS) in 2004 for the study and practice of archives, and a graduate course in archival science (GCAS) at Gakushuin University in 2008, as the only graduate school offering a degree in archival science. During this period, the Japanese government experienced a series of inappropriate problems regarding the management of public records; in particular, the disappearance of pension records caused a social debate. Yasuo Fukuda, who became Prime Minister after serving as Chief Cabinet Secretary, was a statesman with a strong interest in the management of public records, and under his leadership, the Public Records and Archives Management Act was enacted. Although this Act is limited to the management of public records and archives by administrative organizations, it has provided an opportunity to significantly advance the role and status of archives and archivists in Japan.

In Japan, acts and regulations concerning freedom of information and archives have been established step-by-step, however, few professionals actually administer these systems. In addition, the small number of archivists who do exist are mostly in the public sector, and even fewer work in the private sector. The first realistic option for public sector archivists was to solve the problem of "supply" of staff in response to the rapidly increasing "demand" for archivists. To fully realize the education of the profession, the National Archives of Japan, under the strong leadership of its then director, produced a document called "Standard of Tasks and Competencies for Archivist:STCA" with the input of the community involved in archives.

The STCA is a document that describes the relationship between the duties of archivists in the public sector and the professional knowledge and skills required to perform them. It is intended to be used by universities and institutions involved in the education and training of archivists to structure their curricula. It is expected that this will enable professionals who share an intellectual foundation to be trained by several educational and training institutions and play an active role in public records management and archival institutions.

## 7.3 What Did the "STCA" Bring About?

The STCA broadly categorizes the duties of an archivist into four areas: "appraisal, selection, and collection development," "collection management," "provision of public access," and "outreach and communication services." Collection management involves preservation and advocacy is at the heart of communication. In particular, "appraisal" and "outreach and communication services" are areas that have not necessarily been well served by record keeping in Japan, and trained archivists are expected to be able to solve these problems.

One problem with public record management in Japan is that archival institutions have limited influence on parent institutions.

The 2009 Public Records and Archives Management Act provides a front-end approach to archive management similar to that used successfully in Australia's record-keeping system. Archivists at the National Archives provide professional and technical advice to their parent institutions, and similar mechanisms are being modeled on this act in local ordinances, which are becoming more prevalent nationwide. The "STCA" places the involvement of the parent institution from the archival institution as similar to the "appraisal" extended in ISO 15489-1:2016. Furthermore, the conscious development of advocacy for users and stakeholders of archival institutions' services, including "appraisal," in addition to outreach to users of archival materials, should raise the level of Japan's recordkeeping system as a whole.

Moreover, the "STCA" serves as the basis for an official qualification system for archivists, who are at the core of such activities. The National Archives of Japan has begun certifying "certified archivists" from 2020. Although the JSAS had already been conducting a project to register professionals with a certain level of knowledge, skills, and experience and publish a list of such professionals, it was a landmark for a public government agency to establish a certification system on its own. Although the government has been strongly criticized for the scandal involving the management of public records, it has demonstrated a positive attitude toward the training of archivists and has established qualifications that stabilize the existence of the profession; an increasing number of universities are beginning to offer training for archivists. As aforementioned, the clarification of the core elements of the educational curriculum has led to the entry of many universities other than Gakushuin University, which was a pioneer, and the diversification of sources for the profession [Table 7.1].

According to the 2022 survey, in which the National Archives of Japan received responses from 208 initially certified individuals, most had an intellectual background in history. The role of archivists is not only expanding in Japan but it is also expected that people with the ability to meet this demand will be involved in record management and archiving. Those who received certification are people in their 40s to 50s or older who have worked in this field, either before the institution was established or by completing graduate school before the introduction of archival science in Japan. The number of professionals with diverse intellectual backgrounds are expected to increase in the future [Table 7.2].

**Table 7.1** Graduate schools with curricula corresponding to the qualifications of certified archivists

| Name of the Graduate school | Effective Year | Remarks |
|---|---|---|
| Gakushuin University<br>– Graduate Course in Archival Science, Graduate School of Humanities(GCAS) | 2011* | Department |
| Osaka University | 2021 | Course |
| Shimane University<br>– Graduate School of Human and Social Sciences | 2021 | Program |
| Showa Women's University<br>– Graduate School of Life Sciences | 2022 | Program |
| Tohoku University<br>– Graduate School Faculty of Arts and Letters | 2022 | Course |
| Chuo University<br>– Graduate School of Letters | 2023 | Program |
| University of Tsukuba<br>– Graduate School of Comprehensive Human Sciences<br>– Graduate School of Business Sciences, Humanities and Social Sciences | 2023 | Program |
| Beppu University<br>– Graduate School of Humanities | 2024 | Program |

*For the GGAS, which was established before the qualification system was implemented, those educated under the curriculum from 2011 onward are eligible

**Table 7.2** Final major in graduate or undergraduate studies

| | Number | % |
|---|---|---|
| Archival Science | 17 | 8.3% |
| Literature | 8 | 3.9% |
| History | 131 | 63.6% |
| Philosophy | 1 | 0.5% |
| Law, Political Science | 9 | 4.4% |
| Commerce, Economics | 5 | 2.4% |
| Sociology | 6 | 2.9% |
| Science | 1 | 0.5% |
| Engineering | 1 | 0.5% |
| Education | 9 | 4.4% |
| Art | 4 | 1.9% |
| Others | 14 | 6.8% |
| Total | 206 | 100.0% |

Source: National Archives of Japan (2022), Survey result on the status of Certified Archivists, p. 3. [in Japanese]. Breakdown of the 206 respondents.

Concerning the characteristics of records keeping at public institutions in Japan, active involvement in the field of records management is an issue. Most certified archivists work for archival institutions, and few professionals work for parent institutions or the government. In Japan, there are no professionals with the skills to be considered record managers, and archivists must perform some of these roles. In the face of these structural challenges to records keeping in Japan, the "STCA" will be used as a guideline for a common knowledge base for the records profession.

## 7.4 Professional Training and Education

The training of professionals to assist the parent institution in the field of recordkeeping is being pursued primarily through several programs conducted by National Archives rather than by universities. By targeting incumbents in the parent institution and selecting and focusing on resources, they are accelerating the development of recordkeepers who also have contact with archivists. However, short-term programs are limited to familiarizing participants with acts, regulations, and guidelines, and whether a long-term program specializing in record management is necessary or its content remains unclear.

The most comprehensive curriculum is offered by the Graduate Course in Archival Science, Gakushuin University (GCAS), and since its inception in 2008, it has aimed to provide students who wish to become professionals, scholars, or educators in archival science with an education that meets international standards. The GCAS renewed its curriculum in 2021 with the launch of a Certified Archivist system in mind. Its chief focus is to respond to the digital society.

In Japan, as in other countries and regions, the term "Digital Archive" is used by museums and libraries outside the traditional communities involved in archives to describe a system that provides metadata and imaged content data about collections and has spread rapidly in recent years. The 2022 revision of the Museum Act added to the promotion of digital archiving of collections as a museum project. This amendment was made to diversify the modes of museum use in response to the lockdown caused by the COVID-19 pandemic in addition to breakthroughs in digital communication technology. Although cooperating to ensure and enrich the preservation and access to memory heritage is significant for archives, museums, and libraries, archives have the inherent mission of capturing information produced by digital technology as records and ensuring the quality of their management. It is important for archivists to have the knowledge and skills to design the overall picture of such "Digital Archives" in a seamless and consistent recordkeeping process from the parent institution to the archives, and as aforementioned, this is a matter that requires even more attention in Japan, where the relationship with the parent institution has been poor.

Based on this awareness of the problem, the GCAS curriculum renewal revised the information processing seminar to correspond to the knowledge and practice of "Digital Archives," designing and constructing a system of recordkeeping that includes digital records, and enhancing the contents and metadata provision service. Classes were established to address these two scenarios. Clearly, it is essential to update knowledge and skills in a short period in response to the rapid pace of digital technology evolution. The content of education at graduate schools must be reviewed more flexibly than ever before, so that graduates can also use the courses as places to relearn.

From the perspective of encouraging continued learning after graduation, another issue is improving the stability of social environment such that professionals can expect stable employment, job transfers, and career development. The next section introduces the current situation of archivists in Japanese society.

## 7.5 Treatment of Archivists and its Improvement

However, archivists in Japan are not always treated well. In the first survey of certified archivists, the majority (78%) held permanent positions in national archives, whereas less than half held permanent positions in local governments. Considering that one of the requirements for certification is a maximum of five years of work experience, it is possible that those who are not in a post with stable employment are not in a group that meets the requirements for certification in the first place, making it difficult for young people to find a job. In terms of economic standards at the time of the survey, the majority of certified archivists were living on compensation equivalent to the average Japanese annual income, which is insufficient for a profession that requires a master's degree or higher. Similar to other developed countries, Japan's population is rapidly declining. Professions in which the younger generation has no expectation from the future will decline.

The following is a typical example of working as an archivist at a public institution in Japan.

After graduating from university with an undergraduate degree (any major, but often history), students enter graduate school to obtain a master's degree or higher education. Although the type of education and degree received are not strictly required, prospective students who complete certain graduate programs listed in [Table 7.1] with curricula approved by the National Archives with the involvement of a committee that reviews for accreditation begin their job search as "Associate Certified Archivists." Annually, 10–20 openings are available for professional positions at archival institutions, including nonpermanent positions. The "Associate Certified Archivist" program began in 2024, and although it is not yet a requirement to apply for such positions, it is expected to have a favorable effect on hiring decisions.

Associate Certified Archivists hired by archival institutions are prepared for formal certification while also improving their research skills as they acquire three years of work experience. Most Japanese archival institutions are public institutions and function within the framework of a civil service system that has traditionally emphasized generalists. In Japan, there is a tendency for regular job rotations that do not consider the wishes and preferences of individuals, even specialists, making it difficult to develop specialists for specific jobs. However, archivists in small municipal archives institutions are often the "lone arranger," and in addition to being forced to handle a wide range of duties, their workload and lack of opportunities for training and retraining make it similarly difficult for them to develop expertise for career development.

It is noteworthy that those who have not completed a specific graduate program and are not qualified as "Associate Certified Archivists" may receive certification by completing a training program offered by the National Archives or other institutions or by obtaining an evaluation of their competence with a minimum of five years of work experience overall. This is a special exception meant to protect the interests of the generation that began their careers before the certification system was established, and once young people with the will and ability to become archivists have sufficient opportunities to receive a systematic education, the adoption of "Associate Certified Archivist" as a beginning point for their careers will become the principle.

The challenge then becomes how to realize the diversity of archivists as entities. It is difficult to provide a rich education simply by relying on a "STCA" that describes only the minimum content, and there is a risk that the homogenization of the profession will go further than necessary, resulting in a closed recruitment and career system that will make it difficult for innovation to occur in both research and practice.

Furthermore, in order for Japanese archivists, who have often been "reticent" and devoted themselves to being a "custodian," to enter an era in which they will become managers and top executives of archival institutions, it is important to provide them with education even before they enter the profession. "STCA" continues to be at a rudimentary stage and tends to describe only the aspects of knowledge and skills that are readily apparent on the surface. It is necessary to have standards for clarifying and evaluating individual abilities to produce excellent results, as well as professional behavioral characteristics such as personality, motivation, values, and competencies. Such improvements can be accomplished through dialogue and cooperation between archival institutions that employ archivists and educational institutions that prepare young people for professional life, a responsibility that the two institutions owe to the next generation.

## 7.6 Conclusion

Japan experienced a miraculous recovery from the devastation wrought by World War II and its rapid economic growth. Today, standing at a crossroads where it has begun to lose its former prosperity as an "economic superpower," reviewing our own past will help us face the factors that led to such a decline, and ironically, may one day bring Japanese studies back into the limelight.

What is different is that the records to be maintained are not only in analog media, but are now multimedia, including digital records. The knowledge and skills required of archivists are naturally constantly changing, and the standards of the 1980s, when the "Public Archives Act" was established, are far from being at par.

If Japanese society realizes the importance of reviewing the past, rather than merely retrospectively, then it has the opportunity to reiterate the significance of archives and archivists who play an important role in recordkeeping and provide reliable and credible information.

Archivist education in Japan has developed because of the gap between the lack of interest in archives in the political and administrative spheres and the high interest of academic scholars. In Japan, where public history is not well-established, a gap exists between historical scholars and the general public. In the future, it will be necessary for archivists to increase their contact with society and the public. With the spread of digital devices and applications for communication, there are people in the general public who have a certain level of literacy about digital information and have been trained to "doubt" in a positive sense. The first step may be for archival institutions and archivists to obtain public trust through work that can withstand verification from such people.

Professional associations would normally play a central role as a basis for their activities, however, unfortunately, no such organization exists in Japan, where the official qualification system has begun to take effect. Therefore, there is no established code of ethics for archivists, and we can only refer to the ICA's 1996 resolution. In addition, the ICA's code of ethics was expected to inspire public confidence in the profession, however, it is only possible to understand it if one has sufficient knowledge and experience to become a member of the profession. This was evident from the need for the ICA to issue a simple and concise "Universal Declaration on Archives" in 2010.

The "STCA" is a document that defines archivists, their duties, and the knowledge, skills, and competencies required to conduct their responsibilities, primarily for professionals working in public institutions, but not necessarily for the general public. However, this is not necessarily easy for the public to understand.

We must not stop the movement that has begun to advance in the roles and positions of archives and archivists in Japan. We must appeal to the younger generation who may become professionals in the future, even before they read the "STCA," educate them to respond to their sensitivity and awareness of issues. Furthermore, it is an urgent task for the community involved in archives to collaborate to improve the treatment that supports continuous learning and ambition.

[Note]

The National Archives of Japan has published the full text of the "Standard of Tasks and Competencies for Archivist" in English on its website. A Japanese-language commentary by the author of this chapter has also been published.

In addition, the 40th issue (June 2024) of *Journal of the Japan Society of Archival Science*, has a feature article introducing the characteristics of each university's curriculum for "Certified Archivist" education.

# Chapter 8
# Presence of the Calculable: Impacts and Implications of Data Collection in Contemporary Iran

**Satoshi Abe**

**Abstract** The applications of numerical data have been essential features of diverse fields that came to be problematized in Iran since the late nineteenth century. In recent decades, the country has experienced severe environmental problems on various fronts and has been forced to take counter measures in a variety of ways. As a result, the field has become an intensified research investigation site. This chapter examines how the field of the environment is characterized by and problematized through numbers and how such understandings about the environment are distinctively unfolding in several directions; in particular, I argue, they are incorporated into the formation of "environmentally conscious" subjects and are tied to the substantial yet unexpected expansion of infrastructure.

**Keywords** Contemporary Iran · Problematization · Statistics · Visibility and calculability · Numerical data · Environmentally Conscious Subject · Infrastructure

## 8.1 Introduction

Practices of data collection in Iran gradually became common in the late nineteenth century when the country suffered from severe outbreaks of cholera that swept across its territories.[1] Iran's monarch's efforts to contain the disease kept failing due mainly to insufficient resources and management, reportedly resulting in the loss of approximately 10% of its capital's population in 1892 (Afkhami 2019, p. 72). Under these circumstances, the Iranian government—guided by the health protocols of the international community—continuingly attempted to overhaul its dysfunctional

[1] Afkhami (2019) analyzes how Iran's monarch responded to the epidemic from the 1850s through the early 1900s.

S. Abe (✉)
Faculty of Regional Sciences, Tottori University, Tottori, Japan
e-mail: asatoshi@tottori-u.ac.jp



K. Fujiyoshi (ed.), *Governance, Ignorance, and Archives*,
https://doi.org/10.1007/978-981-95-1962-0_8

sanitary programs in order to confront the subsequent cholera epidemics that erupted both domestically and overseas. Although their attempts to curb the spread of the disease were not successful, their employment of statistics for the management of the disease and the protection of the population was one of the early indications that population data was being collected in Iran.[2] Statistical data allowed the authorities to gather information about its population, gave shape to it with numbers, and then subjected the numbers to analysis with the object of management.[3] In other words, what was previously invisible turned into something visible and calculable under the guise of political concerns (Mitchell 2011). The presence of such visibility and calculability is one of the features of modern Iran that continues to proliferate in a variety of fields.

What was remarkable about these developments was the role played by modern science in providing an analytical framework through which experts sought to understand the epidemics and develop preventive measures against them.[4] As Schayegh (2009) demonstrates, Iran's adaptation of modern science accelerated from the first half of the twentieth century, allowing those who govern to gain visibility of and exercise power over its population in a variety of fields. Hacking (1990) points to some analytical implications of modern science's impact on society, arguing that scientists and experts contributed to the rise in importance of numbers and quantification in broader social contexts. It is against the background of the introduction of modern science to Iran that data collection was deemed increasingly relevant and vital for governance. Although the status of modern science remains the subject of debate, especially in Iran's religious communities,[5] many Iranians, religious leaders included, view its intellectual tradition as suitable and qualified for analyzing and providing solutions for social issues.[6]

The environment is one of the disciplinary fields in Iran that has developed based on the schemes of modern science and statistical analyses therefrom. In recent

---

[2] For example, the improvement of the quality of drinking water, public laundries, latrines, and bathhouses was considered a key challenge for the government, which required them to manage underground resources and public spaces (Afkhami 2019, p. 33). Asad (1994, p. 76) notes the growing significance of statistics in non-Western contexts as a political instrument for regulating and transforming populations. See also Appadurai (1993) for similar arguments and analyses in the context of the Indian colonies.

[3] See Schayegh (2009) for his analyses of biopolitics in modern Iran that was gradually becoming a common approach to governance.

[4] Dar al-Fonun, a college known to be the first scientific institution in Iran, was founded in 1851 with an emphasis on the military and technical nature sciences. It offered classes on various scientific disciplines, including medicine, mathematics, and engineering. See Encyclopedia Iranica "DĀR AL-FONŪN" and Ekhtiar (2001) for its development and influence as an educational institution.

[5] Lotfalian (2004) explores how modern science was discussed and received by religious communities in Iran and elsewhere.

[6] Religious leaders in Iran have historically struggled to make sense of scientific knowledge from the viewpoint of their expertise. See for example the works of Arjomand (2020), Gamini (2021), and Rajaee (1993).

decades, Iran has experienced severe environmental problems on multiple fronts—including air, water, soil, and sound—to the extent that they have become policy priorities of the government. Given the growing attention to these problems, this chapter examines how the field of the environment is characterized by and problematized through numbers and how such understandings about the environment are distinctively unfolding in several directions in Iran; in particular, they are incorporated into the formation of "environmentally conscious" subjects and are tied to the substantial yet unexpected expansion of infrastructure. In doing so, the chapter sheds light on some of the fundamental social impacts and implications conditioned by environmental discourses and the employment of numerical data in contemporary Iran.

## 8.2 Emergence of the Field of Environment

Statistics cumulated through data collection concerning the environment has helped define the field, especially after the 1950s when Iran began realizing environment-related problems in the country. Forest management was, for example, an urgent matter of concern for Iran needing to accommodate a growing population, urbanization, and an expanding transportation infrastructure. Although forest management policies had existed previously, it was the arrival of foreign experts in the 1950s that changed the dynamics of forest management in the country with new projects concerning forest conservation, range management, and wood technology (Sadan 2023, pp. 144–145). To confront problematized phenomena, relevant data were gathered such that the forest was rendered more visible and manageable as an object of intervention (Asad 1994); for example, mapping of Iran's forests based on forest density allows policy makers to discern rational uses of the lands and to draft policies therefrom.[7]

In recent decades, environmental concerns have become heightened in a variety of ways, as Iran undergoes rapid population growth, urbanization, and industrialization in the processes of recovering from the Iran–Iraq war, 1980–1988 (Madani 2014). Accordingly, the practice of data collection became increasingly common as a way to identify problems that, as will be shown later, are represented by numbers. Environmental problems concern not just deforestation, but now also issues relating to air, noise, water, and biodiversity. Poor air quality engendered mainly by carbon dioxide emissions from vehicles became literally visible as haze in big cities, reportedly causing respiratory diseases and raising serious health concerns among citizens. Starting from the 1990s in the post-war periods, heavy traffic jams filled with energy-inefficient cars and motorcycles caught the attention of increasing numbers of citizens and policy makers in Iran. In addition, the noise pollution from

[7] Appadurai (2002, p. 639) discusses how mapping can be a powerful tool for communities under scrutiny to organize and mobilize themselves in favor of advancing their own rights, resources, and claims.

unceasing traffic in the streets and nearby industrial sites came to be viewed as another environmental problem.[8] Finally, after years of lower precipitation, a critical shortage of water required for agricultural management and rising water consumption became palpable, triggering heated discussions about effective water use and conservation.[9]

Iran's Five-Year Development Plans over the past several decades feature the country's increasing attention to the environment and display ways in which the environment is defined and problematized as an object of management using numerical data. Every 5 years, Iran announces economic, cultural, and social schemes of development, along with their rationales and follow-up measures to take in the coming years. The Plans reflect and address socioeconomic concerns that need to be dealt with at the time of publication, thus serving as an indicator of the kinds of issues that concern the state at a particular time. The Plans, which were first published under the Islamic Republic right after the end of the Iran–Iraq war in 1989, reveal that the field of the environment has become a distinct calculable object of scientific analysis and has allowed its scope of inquiry to grow by means of calculability. Of various socioeconomical issues in Iran, the Plans reveal that matters of the environment have become more pronounced over time, noticeably by relevant sections getting lengthier and more elaborated (Abe 2018).

It is in this context of increasing problematization of the field in Iran that the environment is understood as an object of systematic management or intervention, for which statistics play a major role. The following statements about environmental measures in the Plan published in 1989, for example, show the typical underlying assumption about the environment: the environment is a calculable object that requires "management" for it to remain healthy.

1. Before the implementation of large industrial projects, research studies concerning environmental feasibility (*emkan sanji*) and locality (*mekan yabi*)—based on the models approved by the Department of Environment (DOE) council—must be conducted.
2. In carrying out any kind of industrial or mining activity, the goals of sustainable development that are framed with environmental standards must be taken into consideration.
3. The country must properly benefit from natural resources while maintaining a balance between the environment's potential and its capacity.

With this conceptual premise that views the environment as calculable and endowed with a certain capacity for sustainable use, numbers provide a key to addressing "environmental problems" and to formulating government policies therefrom. Environmental experts usually discuss Iran's ongoing environmental problems by referencing numbers (with variables) made available through statistics.

[8] https://www.irna.ir/news/85251068/گلایه-مردم-تهران-از-آلودگی-صوتی-راه-علاج-چیست (accessed on May 8, 2025).

[9] https://www.isna.ir/news/1403122014062/واقعیت-تلخ-کم-آبی-تهران-از-کاهش-مخازن-تا-موتورسواری-در-سدها (accessed on May 8, 2025).

In a recent report on the country's water problem in the journal of *Iranian Studies*, for example, Tahbaz (2016, p. 947) explains inadequate uses of domestic water resources with the statistics from Iran's statical center[10]: 92 percent of the water resources is consumed in the agricultural sector when only 9.5 percent of Iran's land area is cultivated. Similarly, drawing on the Food and Agriculture Organization of the United Nations (FAO), he also describes a general scarcity of Iran's water resources with reference to the following variables in tandem with numbers: the country's average precipitation (400 cubic kilometers), annual renewable water sources (137 cubic kilometers), and the amounts of surface and ground water withdrawal (40 and 53.1 cubic kilometers, respectively). This tendency of referencing numbers in assessing the condition of the environment is also evident elsewhere when Tahbaz (2016, p. 950) addresses other environmental problems, such as air pollution, biodiversity, and climate change. Air pollution is problematized in terms of carbon dioxide emissions and dust storms, as these variables are judged to be the major components of the environmental problem. The measurement of biodiversity correlates with those of flora and fauna that "consist of 194 species of mammals, 534 species of birds, 216 species of reptiles, twenty species of amphibians, and 180 species of freshwater fish" found in the country (Tahbaz 2016, p. 954). Habitat destruction and fragmentation are the primary concerns detracting from the healthy state of biodiversity.[11]

Thus, findings suggest that numbers and statistical data provided under the scheme of modern science were conducive to making "environmental problems" calculable and manageable increasingly from the 1950s on in Iran. As environmental problems represented through numbers became tangible and serious after the Iran–Iraq war, more institutions and experts rely on the same kind of statistical data to tackle them and lay out environmental policies (Verran 2010). It is this understanding of the environment that enacts on and is enacted by many Iranians in particular manners that led to the formation of the "environmentally conscious" subject, as will be shown below.

## 8.3 Formation of the Environmentally Conscious Subject

Numbers provided by data collection are central to the organization of environmental discourses among many of my interlocutors.[12] Many Iranians I spoke with—researchers, university students, NGO workers, and non-expert citizens—often

[10] Tahbaz (2016) touches on the roles played by the statistical center of Iran established in 1965 in providing the total population count, as well as population density, with which to identify water stressed regions in the country.

[11] Tahbaz (2016) further includes overgrazing, lack of law enforcement and regulation, poaching, disease, insufficient management and control, pollution, lack of awareness of the laws and regulations, lack of community engagement and participation, and natural hazards.

[12] See Desrosieres (1998) for the idea of "objectification."

mentioned numbers in our conversations when, for example, they described to me the country's environmental plight, emphasized its unique existent biodiversity, or shared their personal stories about environmental initiatives. During my fieldwork in Tehran in 2016, for example, a non-expert park visitor brought up problematic aspects of water use in Iran as follows, when asked about his general view of the country's environmental challenges:

> Recent water problems have become urgent and are felt everywhere due to the mishandling of water resources by the government. They spend 90% of water resources for agriculture, which is disproportionate to the economy, while forcing the entire population to rely on the remaining 10% for their lives. This mishandling has set off critical water shortages.

Here, the statistics concerning water consumption became a point of reference through which his understandings about the environment and its related problems are shaped, organized, and expressed. Similarly, numbers also provide a concrete yardstick by which to assess and address another emerging environmental issue: the degrading state of biodiversity in the country; news outlets typically portray changes in biodiversity in terms of numbers. Referencing the criteria set by the International Union for Conservation of Nature (IUCN), for example, *Tehran Times*, a major English daily newspaper published in Iran, gives an account of Iran's critical state of biodiversity[13]: "Out of 209 mammals, 560 birds, 242 reptiles, and 25 amphibians, some 75 species were included on the IUCN Red List in 2022." It further gives details of the situation by stating "among endangered animal species, bustards and Asiatic cheetahs are in a more critical situation, there are roughly 19 species of bustards and 25 species of cheetahs identified [as being at risk] in the country."

Such ways of thinking and understanding about biodiversity loss fleshed out with numbers are commonly present among environmental activists I spoke with; they usually turn to and make reference to statistical data in the process of deciding how their activities are to proceed. Numbers allow them to identify geographical areas to focus on in the country, target priorities to tackle, and determine methods to be employed. The environmental activists were, for example, well aware that the number of "endangered species" has increased over the past decades in some regions of Iran that, they said, are now in need of protection and conservation: "our country is known to possess a large number of species, especially across the north where the wealth of biodiversity is rapidly disappearing." It is precisely this environment represented through numbers that they tried to deal with by engaging in environmental activities. This environment also offers a framework against which another pressing issue, air pollution, is problematized. Many, if not all, interlocutors recognize that air pollution has become an urgent, everyday problem in urban areas of Iran and that it is mainly caused by gas emissions from vehicles, as well as by dust particles floating from neighboring countries.[14] Apart from the apparent (in)visibility of the air,

---

[13] https://www.tehrantimes.com/news/498592/Some-75-animal-species-in-Iran-on-IUCN-Red-List (accessed on March 27, 2025).

[14] https://www.irna.ir/news/85572255/آلودگی-هوای-پایتخت-افزایش-پدیده-گرد-و-خاک-همزمان-با-آلایندگی (accessed on May 8, 2025).

they come to understand the severity of air pollution usually by scientific measurement of pollutants; the levels of air pollution are rendered calculable and visible by those measurements.[15] The relevant information on the air is regularly updated under the supervision of Iran's DOE and becomes available through various media outlets, such as newspapers, radio, and online news.[16]

Noticeably, religious leaders also generally share this distinct notion of the environment being subject to calculation and management, indicating that they too take in numerical information and see little incongruity with such a notion. By and large, they view no contradiction between Islamic and scientific approaches to the environmental crisis. DOE officials frequently hold meetings with religious leaders of *howzeh*, Shi'i seminaries, discussing ways of dealing with environmental issues in religiously compatible manners.[17] They have also signed Memorandums of Understanding (MOUs) on numerous occasions to mutually address and work out imminent environmental threats.[18] In his well-known book *Islam and Environment*, Ayatollah Javadi-Amoli (2009), a prominent Shi'i scholar, shares such sentiments of compatibility when he argues that humans are bestowed with a right to utilize natural resources to their advantage with the condition that they do not alter the delicate balance of the world originally designed by the divine. Due to its emphatic attention to the sustainable use of natural resources, this conceptual framework is normally deemed compatible with the one that underlies the scientific schemes of sustainable development projects explored above. I had a chance to attend a meeting in 2016 in which scientific experts from the DOE and religious leaders exchanged their ideas about ways to raise environmental awareness in Iran. In the meeting, while backing up their rationales for promoting environmental awareness with authoritative religious texts, they showed support for the DOE's projects to implement scientific management of the environment that places an emphasis on sustainable development (Abe 2021). Research findings suggest that the notion of the environment as being calculable and manageable is generally understood to be nonconflicting and reconcilable for many of Iran's religious leaders.

In our discussions about environmental issues in the country, my interlocutors, regardless of their background, usually postulate a calculable entirety called the environment, against which problems are presented and their solutions are suggested accordingly. Such a particular understanding or use of the notion reveals performative aspects among them, affecting how they view themselves in relation to and how they believe they should act in the environment that is postulated and pursued. Scholars in several disciplines explore performative aspects of language use among their practitioners. Austin (1975), for example, pays attention to the aspect

[15] See the definition of Air Quality Index here: https://www.tabnak.ir/fa/news/1204627/شاخص-آلودگی-هوا-چیست (accessed on May 8, 2025).

[16] https://link.springer.com/article/10.1007/s40201-021-00735-5 (accessed on May 8, 2025).

[17] https://www.isna.ir/news/1401091509889/حوزه-های-علمیه-برای-حفظ-و-حراست-از-محیط-زیست-مشارکت-می-کنند (accessed on May 8, 2025).

[18] For example, see the following link: https://www.isna.ir/news/1403092719720/سازمان-محیط-زیست-و-حوزه-های-علمیه-تفاهم-نامه-همکاری-امضا-کردند (accessed on May 9, 2025).

of language use that is not so much about the conveyance of information in the conventional sense as it is about the actions or accomplishments that are to ensue. Elaborating on Austin's theoretical implications, Derrida (1982) and Butler (1993) explore how our use of language to describe the world or gendered identities critically involves ourselves in transforming the world or making our identities real. In this light, the problematization of the environment enabled by the use of numbers as introduced above can be considered the activity that prompts individuals to act in relation to such environment and thereby to change it into that particular object.

In fact, the problematization of the environment through numbers coincides with the presence of the types of subjects who articulate and act in ways that effectuate the force of calculability on environmental discourses and practices. I have encountered many individuals who fit such description over the course of my fieldwork: those who hear about a high AQI in the news change a plan for an outing to indoor activities or, in another case, decide to delay leaving for work to avoid the bad air; those who study and closely follow the statistics on biodiversity start up environmental activities out of their sincere desire to increase that number; and those who witness water reservoirs in a nearby area shrinking change their ways of water use based on religious discretion, in the faith that exceeding water consumption disrupts the world order created by the divine.

The environmental discourses that I came across in Iran are generally framed within the schemes of modern science and are critically organized through numbers. The DOE and other branches of government have helped produce and circulate such discourses through numerous environmental projects by way of management.[19] Many—environmental activists, non-expert citizens, and religious leaders—adapt and act on these discourses, prompting them to become "environmentally conscious" subjects. Along with these developments, the environment that is discernable with numbers has taken a distinctive turn in the Iranian context, which will be examined in the next section.

## 8.4 Expansion of Infrastructure: A Case of Air Pollution

While data collection concerning the environment conditioned its field to depend on numbers, it also helps in the creation of new infrastructure and in making adjustments to existing infrastructure (Silverstein 2020). Infrastructure constitutes an assemblage of, for example, computers, roads, vehicles, security cameras, institutions, and resources necessary to implement environmental projects. Such an assemblage cannot be entirely reduced to its material dimensions but also reveals important features of the social and the political (Anand 2017; Bowker 2014). This section explores how statistical data for air quality is a crucial part of an assemblage that has

[19] For example, see the following link: https://www.mehrnews.com/news/5648350/-حوزه-های-علمیه-برای-حفظ-و-حراست-از-محیط-زیست-مشارکت-می-کنند (accessed on May 11, 2025).

enabling functions to connect humans, things, and systems in multifarious ways (Larkin 2013). In exploring further implications of expanding infrastructure amid the country's environmental plight, it also looks at some unexpected developments along with the adjustments of the assembled infrastructure (Harvey and Knox 2015).

Given the aggravated, lingering air pollution, the statistical information of which is made public through media outlets on a regular basis, Tehran Municipality has been forced to take environmental measures on various fronts.[20] One example concerns the development of public transportation in the capital, notably the BRT (Bus Rapid Transit), Tehran Metro System, and traffic regulations. Public transportation projects set out in the 1980s to provide an alternative commute to personal vehicles out of environmental consideration.[21] The very first line of the BRT was introduced to Tehran in 2008 and operated between western and eastern parts of the city, allowing its citizens to move from one place to another with less expense and supposedly less environmental footprint. It continues to develop and extended its running distance to about 180 km with 10 lines in 2024, growing 10-fold from the initial phase. This development included the creation of exclusive BRT lanes that markedly run across the city; these exclusive lanes have greatly saved travel time for BRT users, but at the same time can cause traffic congestion and thus travel delays for non-BRT drivers. The contrast of these traffic patterns is highly visible, especially during morning and evening rush hours. Furthermore, Tehran Municipality recently unveiled the first fleet of electric BRTs purchased from China that would operate on three lines in the city, indicating that the environment is continuingly problematic and entangled with growing infrastructure.[22] The development of BRT lines and their exclusive lanes have gradually taken place by giving attention to the social contexts of when and where people tend to gather, what routes they tend to take to get to these destinations, and the scientific data of how much greenhouse gas emissions vehicles would produce.[23] This development demonstrates how the infrastructure installed to improve the city's air quality has caused people, institutions, and materials such as vehicles and lanes to be mobilized and orchestrated in particular manners.

Similar developments are noticeable in another public transportation project: Tehran Metro System. This project also involves humans, things, and institutions in particular manners; the assemblage is made up of public and private institutions, engineers, and statistical analyses on air pollution as well as passengers, among

[20] Tehran Municipality conventionally views the expansion of public transportation as leading to the reduction of traffic and air pollution. See the following link: https://www.isna.ir/news/7909-00684/شهردار-تهران-توسعه-مترو-به-کاهش-آلودگي-هوا-و-ترافيك-مي-انجامد (accessed on May 11, 2025).

[21] See the following link for the short history of public transportation in Tehran: https://www.hamshahrionline.ir/news/754066/ ناوگان-حمل-و-نقل-عمومی-از-دیروز-تا-امروز-هزینه-سفر-با-اتوبوس-های (accessed on May 11, 2025).

[22] https://www.mehrnews.com/news/6394861/آغاز-فعالیت-اتوبوس-های-برق-جدید-در-۳--خط-اتوبوسرانی-تهران-عکس (accessed on April 26, 2025).

[23] See note 18 and the link provided.

many other things.[24] Tehran Municipality commenced the project of creating commuting and subway systems in Tehran. The original proposal was put together prior to the Islamic Revolution, but construction did not start until the 1980s. Having initially started with a commuter line that runs between the capital and its suburbs in 1999, the metro system now extends to 7 lines with 240 km of track and has greatly helped connect major squares and recreational spots.[25]

Another major environmentally conscious project by Tehran Municipality concerns the regulation of traffic, targeting personal vehicles with the intent to lessen pollutants being emitted from them. The municipality implemented the traffic scheme called the "odd- and even-plan" (*tarh-e zouj o fard*) in 2005, in which automobiles, depending on the last digit of the license plate number, are allowed to enter the congested central parts of the city only on alternate days. With the level of air pollution remaining high, new traffic regulations replaced this plan in 2019, confronting air pollution with more comprehensive schemes: "Tehran Traffic Plan" (*tarh-e terafik-e tehran*) and "Tehran Air Pollution Control Plan" (*tarh-e kontrol-e aludegi hava*).[26] These plans control the flow of traffic by limiting citizens' access to wider areas of the city's central zones from Saturday through Thursday. CCTVs operate ubiquitously in major roads to monitor the ins and outs of vehicles in the restricted zones as a way to enforce regulations.[27] In coordination with such measures, the Municipality has developed elaborate online registration systems through which personal information required for entering the restricted zones is filed and processed, which is also a sign of growing infrastructure. Thus, while air pollution represented through statistical data has become widely problematic, it has enabled things and systems to unfold as new forms of infrastructure that move or are moved by trained expertise, institutions, and resources that are necessary to carry out large-scale projects like traffic regulation (Larkin 2013).

At the same time, some unexpected events prompted changes to infrastructure that had coalesced around environmental considerations in Tehran and elsewhere. For example, during the COVID-19 pandemic, the government created and expanded domestic online platforms, offering online classes and teleworking infrastructure on a national scale. Prior to the pandemic, when the use of online platforms was still relatively uncommon, the government was compelled merely to close governmental offices and schools in the event of poor air quality. With the expansion of

[24] https://www.isna.ir/news/7909-00684/شهردار-تهران-توسعه-مترو-به-كاهش-آلودگي-هوا-و-ترافيك-مي-انجامد (accessed on May 11, 2025).

[25] https://behro.co/en/page/1151/Tehran-urban%2D%2D-suburban-railway-co (accessed on April 26, 2025).

[26] The Tehran Traffic Plan controls the flow of traffic into the city's central zone during designated days and hours by restricting and allowing access only to those who purchase entrance tickets in advance. The Tehran Air Pollution Control Plan intends to mitigate the effects of air pollution by granting a limited access (20 days per season for Tehran-plated vehicles and 15 days per person for non-Tehran-plated vehicles) to enter outskirt areas of the central zone during designated days and hours.

[27] https://www.isna.ir/news/1404012009621/اضافه-شدن-۱۵-هزار-دوربین-نظارت-تصویری-به-تهران-تا-پایان-سال (accessed on May 13, 2025).

infrastructure that has assisted Iranians to remotely study or work, however, the closure of offices or schools on such occasions turned into the proliferation of virtual spaces[28]; these changes reveal how the networks of infrastructure can be contingently connected with and expand on the problematization of air quality. Furthermore, in parallel to the increasing opportunities for virtual classes and teleworking, online platforms also began to be utilized for funeral services during the pandemic as burials and their religious rituals are strictly upheld.[29] More recently, online classes that began to be offered during the pandemic are frequently called upon on other occasions, for example, when the country encounters energy shortages and is in need of cutting energy consumption.[30] These cases of growing infrastructure in Tehran and elsewhere feature and reflect the country's important social conditions of discursive assemblages of which air pollution problems are crucially a part.

However, such expansion of infrastructure has also allowed authorities to grant privileged access to achieve their particular ends, illuminating the political dimensions of these developments. For example, in the case of emergencies, not only ambulances but also the vehicles of state officials and the police are authorized to use BRT exclusive lanes when it is judged necessary from their point of view. Also, traffic cameras are put to use to monitor the movement of vehicles not just for environmental considerations, but rather increasingly for security purposes in recent years.[31] Thus, the problematization of air pollution characterized through numbers takes flight in several directions with growing infrastructure that has enabled the movement of humans, things, institutions, and resources contingently and sometimes unexpectedly.

## 8.5 Conclusion

This chapter brought to a focus the social discourses and use of numerical data in the field of the environment in contemporary Iran. The politics of numbers alongside the introduction of modern science began to appear in the late nineteenth century in the country amid the outbreaks of cholera. The applications of numerical data since have been essential features of diverse fields that came to be problematized, including that of the environment. In recent decades, the country has experienced severe environmental problems on various fronts and has been forced to take

[28] https://www.isna.ir/news/1400063123397/سیر-تا-پیاز-کلاس-های-مجازی-در-دوران-کرونا (accessed on May 13, 2025).

[29] https://donya-e-eqtesad.com/بخش-سایت-خوان-62/3794972-رونق-مراسم-ختم-آنلاین-در-فضای-مجازی (accessed on May 13, 2025).

[30] https://www.radiofarda.com/a/iranian-university-classes-have-gone-virtual/33246120.html (accessed on May 13, 2025).

[31] https://www.tasnimnews.com/fa/news/1402/01/20/2877248/اختصاصی-دوربین-های-ثبت-جرائم-رانندگی-موارد-کشف-حجاب-را-هم-ثبت-می-کنند (accessed on May 13, 2025).

counter measures in a variety of ways. As a result, the field has become an intensified research investigation site, transforming it from a previously little-known field into a major one with some distinctive features; environmental scientists collect and analyze statistical data concerning the environment, providing it visibility and calculability and thus facilitating the management of its related problems.

The present work looked at how such problematization of the environment represented through numbers arose and affected the "environmentally conscious" subjects and the ways in which infrastructure has been expanded in several directions. My research findings suggested that many of my interlocuters, whether they are researchers, university students, NGO workers, or non-expert citizens, view the environment to be a numerically calculable and manageable entity. Religious leaders also share such a conceptual framework based on their rationales and find congruity with the efforts by ecological scientists. With such understandings in mind, many Iranians are engaged in practices deemed "environmentally friendly." The expansion of infrastructure was another important social and political feature of the recent problematization of the environment. Air pollution was an exemplary issue through which the environment is problematized with statistical data and for which elaborate infrastructure was installed that connected individuals, things, resources, and systems in variety of ways. The examination of public transportation projects since the late 1980s demonstrated the nature of contingency and peculiarity that is involved with environmental measures initiated by Tehran Municipality. At the same time, the expansion of infrastructure also revealed political dimensions of society, allowing the authorities to facilitate achieving their own agendas.

As the status of modern science becomes prominent among the religious establishment of Iran, the use of numerical data is expected to be more relevant and prestigious, and thus to be applied to many other fields in the future. The recent COVID-19 pandemic displayed such a case in point of proliferation of data while desperately confronting the spread of the disease that claimed the lives of 150,000 Iranians. This chapter I hope presented and provided some context of contemporary Iran in which the politics of large numbers has increasingly become influential, which would also help understand more deeply the country's other pertinent social issues in the past and the present.

## References

Abe S (2018) An anthropological inquiry into emergent discourses and practices of environment in Iran: framing through the idea of translation. Ann Japan Assoc Middle East Stud 34(1):35–62

Abe S (2021) Pursuing moral dimensions of the environment: a study of Islamic tradition in contemporary Iran. J the Study Relig Nat Cult 15(2):151–176

Afkhami A (2019) A modern contagion: imperialism and public health in Iran's age of Cholera. Johns Hopkins University Press, Baltimore

Anand N (2017) Hydraulic city: water and the infrastructures of citizenship in Mumbai. Duke University Press, Durham

Appadurai A (1993) Number in the colonial imagination. In: Breckenridge CA, van der Veer P (eds) Orientalism and the Postcolonial Predicament. University of Pennsylvania, Philadelphia, pp 314–340
Appadurai A (2002) Why enumeration counts. Environ Urbaniz 24(2):639–641
Arjomand K (2020) Islamic responses to Darwinism in the Persianate World. In: Brown CM (ed) Asian religious responses to Darwinism: modern evolutionary theories in Middle Eastern, South Asian, and East Asian cultural contexts. Springer, Cham, pp 65–89
Asad T (1994) Ethnographic representation, statistics, and modern power. Soc Res 61(1):55–88
Austin JL (1975) How to do things with words, 2nd edn. Havard University Press, Cambridge
Bowker GC (2014) All together now: synchronization, speed, and the failure of narrativity. Hist Theory 53:563–576
Butler J (1993) Bodies that matter: on the discursive limits of "Sex.". Routledge, New York
Derrida J (1982) Margins of philosophy. University of Chicago Press, Chicago
Desrosieres A (1998) The politics of large numbers: a history of statistical reasoning. Harvard University Press, Cambridge
Ekhtiar M (2001) Nasir al-Din Shah and the Dar al-Funun: the evolution of an institution. Iran Stud 34(1/4):153–163
Encyclopedia Iranica. "DĀR AL-FONŪN."
Gamini A-M (2021) A critique of Darwin's *The Descent of Man* by a Muslim Scholar in 1912: Muḥammad-Riḍā Iṣfahānī's examination of the anatomical and embryological similarities between human and other animals. Journal of the History of Biololgy 54(3):485–511
Hacking I (1990) *The taming of chance*. Cambridge University Press, Cambridge
Harvey P, Knox H (2015) Enchantments of infrastructure. Mobilities 7(4):1–16
Javadi-Amoli A (2009) *Eslam va Mohit-e Zist*. Markaz-e Nashr-e Esra, Tehran
Larkin B (2013) The politics of poetics of infrastructure. Ann Rev Anthropol 42:327–343
Lotfalian M (2004) Islam, technoscientific identities, and the culture of curiosity. University Press of America, Lanham
Madani K (2014) Water management in Iran: what is causing the looming crisis. J Environ Stud Sci 4(4):315–328
Mitchell T (2011) Carbon democracy: political power in the age of oil. Verso, London and New York
Rajaee F (1993) Islam and modernity: the reconstruction of an alternative Shiite Islamic Worldview in Iran. In: Marty ME, Appleby RS (eds) Fundamentalisms and society: reclaiming the sciences, the family, and education. University of Chicago Press, Chicago, pp 103–125
Sadan A (2023) Masters of the garden: an environmental history of nation-building in Pahlavi Iran. Doctoral Dissertation. University of Michigan
Schayegh C (2009) Who is knowledgeable is strong: science, class, and the formation of Modern Iranian Society, 1900-1950. University of California Press, Berkeley
Silverstein B (2020) The social lives of numbers: statistics, reform and the remaking of rural life in Turkey. Palgrave Macmillan, Singapore
Tahbaz M (2016) Environmental challenges in today's Iran. Iran Stud 49(6):943–961
Verran H (2010) Number as an inventive frontier in knowing and working Australia's water resources. Anthropol Theory 10(1–2):171–178

MIX
Papier aus verantwortungsvollen Quellen
Paper from responsible sources
FSC® C105338

If you have any concerns about our products,
you can contact us on
**ProductSafety@springernature.com**

In case Publisher is established outside the EU,
the EU authorized representative is:
**Springer Nature Customer Service Center GmbH**
**Europaplatz 3, 69115 Heidelberg, Germany**

Printed by Libri Plureos GmbH
in Hamburg, Germany